W9-CHM-528

Gooseberry patch

From our Kitchen to Yours

Our Best
Farm-Fresh
Recipes

Delicious dishes
for every meal!

To cooks everywhere who want to create easy & delicious farm-fresh dishes for their family & friends.

Gooseberry Patch
An imprint of Globe Pequot
246 Goose Lane
Guilford, CT 06437

www.gooseberrypatch.com
1 800 854 6673

Copyright 2020, Gooseberry Patch
978-1-62093-421-0

All rights reserved. No part of this book may be reproduced or utilized in any form or by any means, electronic or mechanical, including photocopying and recording, or by any information storage and retrieval system, without permission in writing from the publisher.
Printed in United States of America

....

Do you have a tried & true recipe... tip, craft or memory that you'd like to see featured in a **Gooseberry Patch** cookbook? Visit our website at www.gooseberrypatch.com and follow the easy steps to submit your favorite family recipe.

Or send them to us at:
Gooseberry Patch
PO Box 812
Columbus, OH 43216-0812

Don't forget to include the number of servings your recipe makes, plus your name, address, phone number and email address. If we select your recipe, your name will appear right along with it... and you'll receive a FREE copy of the book!

CONTENTS

Farm-Fresh Year 'Round
4

:::::::::::::::::::::::::

Good Morning Sunrise
6

Time for Lunch
68

Coffee-Time Treats
124

Come to Dinner
154

Nibbles & Sips
202

Relax with Dessert
224

:::::::::::::::::::::::::

Index 250

Farm-Fresh Year 'Round

Wherever you live, you will find fresh, local ingredients specific to your area that are available during certain times of the year. Before you choose your recipe, think of the produce that is in season at farmers' markets or in abundance at the supermarket. Even though different parts of the country have different growing seasons and much produce is shipped from overseas, each season still offers produce that is specific to that time of year. Of course, dairy, protein and grains are available year 'round and those ingredients are a must for many recipes. By planning ahead with your recipe choices to include ingredients that are in season, your menus will always be delicious and farm-fresh.

WHEN IS IT IN SEASON?

Good cooking starts with fresh ingredients. When choosing produce, it is helpful to know what ingredients are in season. Here is a list of various kinds of produce and when they are most available. This will help you choose the recipes you want to serve.

WINTER SEASON
- Chestnuts
- Grapefruit
- Kale
- Leeks
- Lemons
- Oranges
- Radicchio
- Radishes
- Rutabagas
- Tangerines
- Turnips

SPRING SEASON
- Apricots
- Artichokes
- Asparagus
- Avocados
- Broccoli
- Cabbage
- Carrots
- Celery
- Cherries
- Chives
- Collards
- Fennel
- Lettuce
- Mangoes
- Morels
- Mustard Greens
- Pineapple
- Rhubarb
- Strawberries
- Spinach
- Swiss Chard

SUMMER SEASON
- Beets
- Blackberries
- Blueberries
- Cantaloupe
- Corn
- Cucumbers
- Green Beans
- Nectarines
- Peaches
- Plums
- Raspberries
- Sweet Peppers
- Tomatoes
- Watermelon
- Zucchini

FALL SEASON
- Acorn Squash
- Almonds
- Apples
- Bananas
- Butternut Squash
- Cauliflower
- Cranberries
- Figs
- Garlic
- Ginger
- Grapes
- Mushrooms
- Pears
- Peanuts
- Pomegranates
- Potatoes
- Pumpkins

Peanut Butter Muffins

CHAPTER ONE

Good Morning Sunrise

Welcome the day with a breakfast that will
make your morning shine.

Fluffy Baked Eggs, Page 16

Oatmeal Waffles, Page 62

Megan Brooks, Antioch, TN

After-Church Egg Muffins

I whip these up for my boys almost every Sunday after church...they start asking for them right when we get home!

Serves 4

10-3/4 oz. can Cheddar cheese soup
1-1/2 c. milk
4 eggs
4 slices Canadian bacon
4 English muffins, split and toasted
4 t. butter, divided

In a bowl, mix together soup and milk. Fill 4 greased custard cups 1/4 full with soup mixture. Set cups on a baking sheet. Crack an egg into each cup, being careful not to break the yolks. Bake cups at 350 degrees for 12 minutes. Meanwhile, brown both sides of bacon in a skillet over medium heat. Top each muffin half with one teaspoon butter. Place 4 muffin halves on a baking sheet. Top each with a slice of bacon. Turn out a baked egg onto each bacon-topped muffin half. Drizzle remaining cheese sauce over each egg. Top with other halves of muffins. Bake for an additional 2 minutes, or until heated through.

Jill Ball, Highland, UT

Apple Pie Oatmeal

This is an easy, healthy and hearty breakfast. Sprinkle a little cinnamon and sugar on top for extra sweetness in the morning.

Makes one serving

1 c. water
6 T. long-cooking oats, uncooked
1 t. brown sugar, packed
2 T. apple, peeled, cored and diced
1/8 t. apple pie spice
Optional: milk

Combine water and oats in a microwave-safe bowl. Cover tightly with plastic wrap, folding back a small edge to allow steam to escape. Microwave on high for 2-1/2 minutes. Stir well. Top with remaining ingredients and milk, if desired.

Apple Pie Oatmeal

Jo Ann, Gooseberry Patch

Blueberry-Lemon Crepes

A scrumptious and refreshing breakfast!

Makes 6 servings

3-oz. pkg. cream cheese, softened
1-1/2 c. half-and-half
1 T. lemon juice
3-3/4 oz. pkg. instant lemon pudding
   mix
1/2 c. biscuit baking mix
1 egg, beaten
6 T. milk
1 c. blueberry pie filling

Combine cream cheese, half-and-half, lemon juice and dry pudding mix in a bowl. Beat with an electric mixer on low speed for 2 minutes. Refrigerate for 30 minutes. Lightly grease a 6" skillet and place over medium-high heat. In a bowl, combine biscuit baking mix, egg and milk. Beat until smooth. Pour 2 tablespoons of batter into skillet for each crepe. Rotating the skillet quickly, allow batter to cover the bottom of the skillet. Cook each crepe until lightly golden, then flip, cooking again until just golden. Spoon 2 tablespoonfuls of cream cheese mixture onto each crepe and roll up. Top with remaining cream cheese mixture and pie filling.

Sonna Johnson, Goldfield, IA

Cranberry Applesauce Muffins

I like to make these by the dozen and take them to church for after-church coffee.

Makes 2 dozen

1 c. fresh or frozen cranberries
1-1/4 c. unsweetened applesauce
1/3 c. canola oil
1 egg, beaten
2 c. all-purpose flour
1/2 c. sugar
1 t. baking soda
1 t. cinnamon
1/2 t. salt

Using a food processor, process cranberries until chopped. Set aside. In a small bowl, mix applesauce, oil and egg. In a large bowl, combine flour, sugar, baking soda, cinnamon and salt. Make a well in the flour mixture. Slowly pour in applesauce mixture, stirring until just moistened. Fold in cranberries. Fill 24 greased or paper-lined muffin cups 2/3 full. Bake at 350 degrees for 25 to 30 minutes, until a wooden toothpick inserted in the center comes out clean. Cool for 2 minutes before removing from cups.

Cranberry Applesauce Muffins

Deborah Wells, Broken Arrow, OK

Cheese & Chive Scrambled Eggs

Paired with hot biscuits, this makes a great breakfast for any day of the week!

Serves 2 to 3

6 eggs, beaten
1/4 t. lemon pepper
1 T. fresh chives, chopped
1/8 t. salt
1 T. butter
1/3 c. shredded Colby Jack cheese
1/3 c. cream cheese, softened

In a bowl, combine eggs, pepper, chives and salt; set aside. Melt butter in a skillet over medium-low heat; add egg mixture. Stir to scramble, cooking until set. Remove from heat; stir in cheeses until melted.

Good News
Eggs are an excellent source of protein, vitamin A and choline, and a good source of folate, so enjoy!

Christina Mendoza, Alamogordo, NM

California Omelet

Always a special breakfast, omelets make the quickest and heartiest breakfasts for the entire family...you can personalize each one to include favorite flavors.

Serves 2

1 T. oil
3 to 4 eggs, beaten
1/4 c. milk
salt and pepper to taste
1 avocado, peeled, pitted and sliced
2 green onions, diced
1/2 c. shredded Monterey jack
    cheese

Heat oil in a skillet over medium-low heat. Whisk together eggs, milk, salt and pepper in a bowl; pour into skillet. Cook until eggs are lightly golden on bottom and partially set on top. Sprinkle with remaining ingredients; carefully fold omelet in half so toppings are covered. Reduce heat and cook, uncovered, about 5 to 10 minutes.

California Omelet

Elizabeth Holcomb, Canyon Lake, TX

Texas Toads in the Hole

I made this recipe for my girls when they were little. They always loved it because of the funny name, as well as the fact they had eggs and toast all in one dish!

Serves 4

2 T. butter
4 slices Texas toast
4 eggs
salt and pepper to taste
Optional: jam, jelly or preserves

Spread butter on both sides of Texas toast. Using a biscuit cutter, cut a circle out of the middle of each slice of toast; set aside rounds. Place toast slices in a large, lightly greased skillet over medium heat; break an egg into each hole. Season with salt and pepper. Cook until egg white begins to set, then carefully flip. Continue to cook until eggs reach desired doneness. In a separate skillet, toast reserved bread rounds. Top rounds with jam, jelly or preserves, if desired. Serve with toast slices.

Paula Johnson, Center City, MN

Cinnamon-Pumpkin Pancakes

Everyone loves this cinnamon and pumpkin combination. Yum!

Makes 2 dozen, serves 6

1 c. whole-wheat flour
1 T. sugar
2 t. baking powder
1/4 t. salt
1/2 t. cinnamon
1 c. skim milk
1/2 c. canned pumpkin
2 eggs, separated and divided
1-1/2 T. oil

In a large mixing bowl, combine flour, sugar, baking powder, salt and cinnamon. In a separate bowl, blend together milk, pumpkin, beaten egg yolks and oil. Add pumpkin mixture to flour mixture all at once, stirring until just blended. Beat egg whites with an electric mixer on high speed until stiff peaks form, then gently fold into pancake batter. For each pancake, spoon 2 to 3 tablespoons batter onto a griddle sprayed with non-stick vegetable spray. Cook until bubbles begin to form around edges; turn and cook until second side is golden.

Cinnamon-Pumpkin Pancakes

Penny Sherman, Cumming, GA

Grab & Go Breakfast Cookies

These cookies are perfect for those busy mornings when you have to rush out the door.

Makes 1-1/2 dozen

1/2 c. butter, softened
1/2 c. sugar
1 egg, beaten
2 T. frozen orange juice concentrate, thawed
1 T. orange zest
1-1/4 c. all-purpose flour
1 t. baking powder
1/2 c. wheat & barley cereal

Blend together butter and sugar in a bowl until light and fluffy. Beat in egg, orange juice and zest; set aside. Combine flour and baking powder in a small bowl; stir into butter mixture until blended. Stir in cereal. Drop by tablespoonfuls, 2 inches apart, on an ungreased baking sheet. Bake at 350 degrees for 10 to 12 minutes, until golden around edges. Cool on a wire rack.

Amy Butcher, Columbus, GA

Fluffy Baked Eggs

Who would have thought to combine pineapple and eggs? After you taste this yummy recipe, you'll see why it is our family favorite!

Makes 12 servings

14 eggs, beaten
3 slices bacon, crisply cooked and crumbled
1-1/3 c. low-fat cottage cheese
8-oz. can crushed pineapple in juice, drained
1 t. vanilla extract
Garnish: cooked bacon crumbles, chopped fresh parsley

Blend together eggs, bacon, cottage cheese, pineapple and vanilla; spoon into a greased 13"x9" baking pan. Bake, uncovered, at 350 degrees for 40 to 45 minutes, until center is set and a toothpick inserted in center comes out clean. Allow baking pan to stand 5 minutes before slicing. Garnish with cooked bacon crumbles and parsley as desired; cut into squares.

Fluffy Baked Eggs

Kristie Rigo, Friedens, PA

Blueberry Pillows

A delightful blend of cream cheese and blueberries are stuffed inside this French toast.

Serves 8

8-oz. pkg. cream cheese, softened
16 slices Italian bread
1/2 c. blueberries
2 eggs, beaten
1/2 c. milk
1 t. vanilla extract

Spread cream cheese evenly on 8 bread slices; arrange blueberries in a single layer over cream cheese. Top with remaining bread slices, gently pressing to seal; set aside. Whisk together eggs, milk and vanilla in a small bowl; brush over bread slices. Arrange on a greased hot griddle; cook until golden. Flip and cook other side until golden.

Nicole Millard, Mendon, MI

Grandma McKindley's Waffles

You can't go wrong with an old-fashioned waffle breakfast...the topping choices are endless!

Makes 8 to 10 waffles

2 c. all-purpose flour
1 T. baking powder
1/4 t. salt
2 eggs, separated
1-1/2 c. milk
3 T. butter, melted
Garnish: fresh berries, maple syrup

Sift together flour, baking powder and salt; set aside. With an electric mixer on high speed, beat egg whites until stiff peaks form; set aside. Stir egg yolks, milk and melted butter together and add to flour mixture, stirring just until moistened. Fold in egg whites. Ladle batter by 1/2 cupfuls onto a lightly greased preheated waffle iron; bake according to manufacturer's directions. Garnish as desired.

Grandma McKindley's Waffles

Sarah Lundvall, Ephrata, PA

Cranberry Hootycreek Pancakes

This is my take on a favorite cookie recipe...for breakfast. My 2-year-old gobbles them up faster than I can make them.

Serves 4

1/2 c. all-purpose flour
1/2 c. quick-cooking oats, uncooked
1 T. sugar
1 t. baking powder
1/2 t. baking soda
1/2 t. salt
1 t. vanilla extract
3/4 c. buttermilk
2 T. oil
1 egg, beaten
1/2 c. white chocolate chips
1/2 c. sweetened dried cranberries

In a bowl, mix flour, oats, sugar, baking powder, baking soda and salt. Add vanilla, buttermilk, oil and egg; stir until well blended. Stir in white chocolate chips and cranberries. In a large, lightly greased griddle over medium heat, drop the batter by 1/4 cupfuls. Cook for about 3 minutes, until tops start to form bubbles. Flip and cook 2 additional minutes, or until both sides are golden.

Jennifer Hansen, Escanaba, MI

Sunrise Granola

Carry this with you on an early morning hike!

Serves 4

1 c. long-cooking oats, uncooked
1/4 c. unsweetened flaked coconut
2 T. sunflower seeds
1/4 c. wheat germ
1/4 t. cinnamon
1 T. honey
1/4 t. vanilla extract
2 t. canola oil

In a large mixing bowl, combine oats, coconut, sunflower seeds, wheat germ and cinnamon. In a separate bowl, combine honey, vanilla and oil; blend well. Pour honey mixture into oat mixture; blend well. Spread on a baking sheet and bake at 350 degrees for 20 to 25 minutes, stirring every 5 minutes. Let cool, then store in an airtight jar.

Flavor Variation

Granola can be made to fit your favorite ingredients. Add rolled wheat, pecans, raisins, dried cranberries or whatever you like to make your granola your own.

Sunrise Granola

Robin Hill, Rochester, NY

Warm Country Gingerbread Waffles

Serve with brown sugar, powdered sugar, hot maple syrup or raspberries.

Makes nine 4-inch waffles

2 c. all-purpose flour
1 t. cinnamon
1/2 t. ground ginger
1/2 t. salt
1 c. molasses
1/2 c. butter
1-1/2 t. baking soda
1 c. buttermilk
1 egg, beaten

Combine flour, cinnamon, ginger and salt. Heat molasses and butter in a saucepan over low heat until butter melts. Remove from heat and stir in baking soda. Add buttermilk and egg; fold in flour mixture. Cook in a preheated greased waffle iron according to manufacturer's instructions.

Amy Tucker, British Columbia, Canada

Peanut Butter Muffins

These will become your family's favorite muffins. They are so moist and full of peanut-buttery flavor!

Makes 1-1/2 dozen

1 c. whole-wheat flour
1 c. long-cooking oats, uncooked
1-1/2 t. baking soda
1/4 c. creamy peanut butter
1/3 c. applesauce
1-1/2 c. skim milk
1/4 c. honey
2 T. finely chopped peanuts

Whisk together flour, oats and baking soda. Add peanut butter and applesauce; beat with an electric mixer on low speed until smooth. Stir in milk and honey. Spoon batter into paper-lined or greased muffin cups, filling 2/3 full. Sprinkle with chopped peanuts. Bake at 350 degrees for 12 to 15 minutes, until a toothpick tests clean. Cool in pan 5 minutes; transfer to a wire rack to finish cooling.

Peanut Butter Muffins

Dale Duncan, Waterloo, IA

Rise & Shine Sandwiches

My family loves breakfast sandwiches for dinner. They're easy to make and easy to adapt to your own tastes!

Makes 8 servings

2-1/4 c. buttermilk biscuit
    baking mix
1/2 c. water
8 pork sausage breakfast patties
8 eggs, beaten
1 T. butter
salt and pepper to taste
8 slices American cheese

In a bowl, combine biscuit mix with water until just blended. Turn onto a floured surface and knead for one minute. Roll dough out to 1/2-inch thickness. Cut out 8 biscuits with a 3-inch round biscuit cutter. Arrange on an ungreased baking sheet. Bake at 425 degrees for 8 to 10 minutes, until golden. Meanwhile, in a skillet over medium heat, brown and cook sausage patties; drain. In a separate skillet over low heat, scramble eggs in butter to desired doneness; season with salt and pepper. Split biscuits; top each biscuit bottom with a sausage patty, a spoonful of eggs and a cheese slice. Add biscuit tops and serve immediately.

Mary Ann Lewis, Olive Branch, MS

Best-Ever Breakfast Bars

These chewy, healthy bars are perfect to grab in the morning for a delicious take-along breakfast.

Makes one dozen

1 c. Sunrise Granola (see page 20)
1 c. quick-cooking oats, uncooked
1/2 c. all-purpose flour
1/4 c. brown sugar, packed
1/8 t. cinnamon
1/2 c. unsalted mixed nuts, coarsely
    chopped
1/2 c. dried fruit, chopped into small
    pieces
2 T. ground flaxseed meal
1/4 c. canola oil
1/3 c. honey
1/2 t. vanilla extract
1 egg, beaten

Combine prepared granola and next 7 ingredients in a large bowl. Whisk together oil, honey and vanilla; stir into granola mixture. Add egg; stir to blend. Press mixture into a parchment paper-lined 8"x8" baking pan. Bake at 325 degrees for 30 to 35 minutes, until lightly golden around the edges. Remove from oven and cool 30 minutes to one hour. Slice into bars.

Best-Ever Breakfast Bars

Ashlee Haefs, Buna, TX

Red Velvet Pancakes

Red velvet cake is one of my family's favorites, so with this recipe we can have it for breakfast...what a great way to start the day!

Makes one dozen pancakes

1-1/2 c. all-purpose flour
2 T. baking cocoa
4 t. sugar
1-1/2 t. baking powder
1/2 t. baking soda
1 t. cinnamon
1 t. salt
2 eggs, beaten
1-1/4 c. buttermilk
1 T. red food coloring
1-1/2 t. vanilla extract
1/4 c. butter, melted
Optional: maple syrup, butter,
    whipped cream cheese

In a bowl, whisk together flour, cocoa, sugar, baking powder, baking soda, cinnamon and salt. In a separate bowl, mix eggs, buttermilk, food coloring and vanilla. Add to flour mixture and mix well. Fold in melted butter. Using an ice cream scoop, drop batter onto a lightly greased, hot griddle and cook until edges darken, about 5 minutes. Flip and cook until done. Serve topped with syrup and butter or whipped cream cheese.

Lois Hobart, Stone Creek, OH

Lemon-Rosemary Zucchini Bread

This zucchini bread is the best! It smells wonderful while it bakes and tastes so good. Mini loaves or muffins make a nice gift.

Makes 2 loaves or 2 dozen muffins

3 c. all-purpose flour
1/2 t. baking powder
2 t. baking soda
2 T. fresh rosemary, minced
2 eggs
1-1/4 c. sugar
1/2 c. butter, melted and slightly
    cooled
1/4 c. olive oil
1 T. lemon zest
3 c. zucchini, grated

In a bowl, whisk together flour, baking powder, baking soda and rosemary; set aside. In a separate large bowl, beat eggs until frothy; beat in sugar, melted butter and olive oil. Stir in lemon zest and zucchini. Add flour mixture to egg mixture; stir until blended. Divide batter into two 9"x4" loaf pans sprayed with non-stick vegetable spray. Bake at 350 degrees for 45 to 50 minutes. May also spoon batter into 24 paper-lined muffin cups, filling 2/3 full; bake at 350 degrees for 20 minutes.

Lemon-Rosemary Zucchini Bread

Cherylann Smith, Efland, NC

Herbed Sausage Quiche

Serve this quiche right from the table...yummy served with fresh fruit.

Makes 8 servings

9-inch frozen pie crust, thawed
1 c. ground pork breakfast sausage, browned and drained
3 eggs, beaten
1 c. 2 % milk
1 c. shredded Cheddar cheese
1 sprig fresh rosemary, chopped
1-1/2 t. Italian seasoning
1/4 t. salt
1/4 t. pepper

Bake pie crust according to package directions. Mix together remaining ingredients in a bowl; spread into baked crust. Bake, uncovered, at 450 degrees for 15 minutes. Reduce oven temperature to 350 degrees, cover with aluminum foil and bake 9 more minutes. Cut into wedges to serve.

Julie Perkins, Anderson, IN

Peanut Butter French Toast

Who can resist the classic taste of peanut butter & jelly?

Serves 2

4 slices white bread
1/2 c. creamy peanut butter
2 T. grape jelly
3 eggs, beaten
1/4 c. milk
2 T. butter
Garnish: powdered sugar

Use bread, peanut butter and jelly to make 2 sandwiches; set aside. In a bowl, whisk together eggs and milk. Dip each sandwich into egg mixture. Melt butter in a non-stick skillet over medium heat. Add sandwiches to skillet and cook until golden, about 2 to 3 minutes on each side. Sprinkle with powdered sugar; cut diagonally into triangles.

Peanut Butter French Toast

Jennifer Howard, Santa Fe, NM

Breezy Brunch Skillet

Try this all-in-one breakfast on your next camp-out! Just set the skillet on a grate over hot coals.

Serves 4 to 6

6 slices bacon, diced
6 c. frozen diced potatoes
3/4 c. green pepper, chopped
1/2 c. onion, chopped
1 t. salt
1/4 t. pepper
4 to 6 eggs
1/2 c. shredded Cheddar cheese

In a large cast-iron skillet over medium-high heat, cook bacon until crisp. Drain and set aside, reserving 2 tablespoons drippings in skillet. Add potatoes, green pepper, onion, salt and pepper to drippings. Cook and stir for 2 minutes. Cover and cook for about 15 minutes, stirring occasionally, until potatoes are golden and tender. With a spoon, make 4 to 6 wells in potato mixture. Crack one egg into each well, taking care not to break the yolks. Cover and cook over low heat for 8 to 10 minutes, until eggs are completely set. Sprinkle with cheese and crumbled bacon.

Carol Field Dahlstrom, Ankeny, IA

Bacon-Corn Muffins

Little bits of crisp bacon make these muffins a breakfast favorite.

Makes 2 dozen

2-3/4 c. all-purpose flour
3/4 c. sugar
2/3 c. yellow cornmeal
1 t. salt
1 t. baking powder
1/2 t. baking soda
1 c. crisply cooked bacon, cut or
    broken into 1/4-inch pieces
1-1/2 c. buttermilk
4 eggs, beaten
3/4 c. oil
2/3 c. shredded Cheddar cheese
1/4 c. red or orange sweet peppers,
    chopped

In a large bowl, combine flour, sugar, cornmeal, salt, baking powder, baking soda and bacon. Make a well in the dry ingredients. Set aside. In a small bowl, mix buttermilk, eggs and oil. Slowly pour egg mixture into flour mixture, stirring until just moistened. Fold in cheese and peppers. Spoon batter into 24 paper-lined or greased muffin cups, filling 3/4 full. Bake at 375 degrees for 20 to 25 minutes, until golden and firm in the center.

Bacon-Corn Muffins

Pam Hooley, LaGrange, IN

Stir & Go Biscuits & Sausage Gravy

This is a quick, stick-to-your-ribs breakfast to start the day. Since finding this recipe for biscuits made with oil, rather than shortening, I make them more often, and the gravy is so easy to make too.

Serves 4 to 6

2 c. all-purpose flour
2-1/2 t. baking powder
1/8 t. baking soda
1 t. sugar
1 t. salt
1 c. buttermilk
1/2 c. oil
Garnish: melted butter

In a large bowl, stir together flour, baking powder, baking soda, sugar and salt. Add buttermilk and oil; stir until moistened. Roll out dough on a floured surface. Cut dough with a biscuit cutter, or drop dough by 1/2 cupfuls, onto an ungreased baking sheet. Bake at 425 degrees for 15 minutes; brush with butter. While biscuits are baking, make Sausage Gravy. Serve gravy over hot biscuits.

SAUSAGE GRAVY
1 lb. ground pork breakfast sausage
2 T. all-purpose flour
1/2 c. milk
salt and pepper to taste

Brown sausage in a skillet over medium heat. Drain; stir in flour until mixed well. Add milk; cook and stir until thickened. May add more milk to desired consistency. Season with salt and pepper.

Patricia Reitz, Winchester, VA

Blueberry Flaxseed Smoothies

This is a healthy and low-calorie way to start your day...and delicious too!

Serves 4

1 banana, cut into chunks
1/2 c. blueberries
1 c. low-fat vanilla yogurt
1 c. fat-free milk
2 T. ground flaxseed
Garnish: fresh strawberries,
    blueberries, flaxseed

Combine all ingredients except garnish in a blender; process on high setting until smooth. Pour into glasses. Garnish with fruit and flaxseed.

Blueberry Flaxseed Smoothies

Beth Kramer, Port Saint Lucie, FL

Strawberry-Hazelnut Grits

This combination of strawberry, cocoa and hazelnut is just too yummy to pass up!

Serves 2

3/4 c. quick-cooking grits, uncooked
1 T. butter
3 T. chocolate-hazelnut spread
6 to 7 strawberries, hulled and
    chopped

Prepare grits according to package directions. Stir in butter and chocolate-hazelnut spread. Fold in strawberries.

Flavor Variation

If another berry is your favorite, substitute blueberries or raspberries for the strawberries. It is yummy with any berry!

Natasha Morris, Ulysses, KS

Egg Casserole Deluxe

This recipe is so versatile! My youngest daughter made this for her sister's bridal shower...it was a big hit with the bride-to-be and the guests! For a crowd, simply double the recipe and bake in a 13"x9" baking pan. We love it for a weekend breakfast. For a quick weeknight dinner, just add a fruit salad and dinner is done!

Serves 8

1 to 2 T. butter
1/2 c. sliced mushrooms
1 doz. eggs, beaten
8-oz. container sour cream
1/2 c. shredded Cheddar cheese
2.8-oz. pkg. pre-cooked bacon,
    crumbled and divided

Melt butter in a large skillet over medium heat. Sauté mushrooms. Add eggs; cook and stir until softly scrambled. Stir in sour cream, cheese and half of bacon. Transfer to a lightly greased 8"x8" baking pan. Sprinkle remaining bacon on top. Bake, uncovered, at 350 degrees for 30 minutes.

Egg Casserole Deluxe

Debi DeVore, New Philadelphia, OH

Maple Hot Chocolate

On cold winter days we like to start the day with hot chocolate. The maple flavoring makes it extra special!

Makes 4 servings

3 T. sugar
1 T. baking cocoa
1/8 t. salt
1/4 c. hot water
1 T. butter
4 c. milk
1 t. maple flavoring
1 t. vanilla extract
12 marshmallows, divided

Combine sugar, cocoa and salt in a large saucepan. Stir in hot water and butter; bring to a boil over medium heat. Add milk, maple flavoring, vanilla and 8 marshmallows. Heat mixture through, stirring occasionally, until marshmallows are melted. Ladle into 4 mugs; top with remaining marshmallows.

Michelle Case, Yardley, PA

Breakfast Berry Parfait

Choose a simple glass dish to present this super-easy breakfast. Or for a fancier look, serve it in parfait glasses or champagne flutes. Choose the flavor of yogurt that your family loves...it all tastes so good!

Makes 3 servings

3/4 c. strawberries, hulled
1/2 c. raspberries
1/4 c. blackberries
1 c. bran & raisin cereal
6-oz. container strawberry yogurt
Garnish: additional fresh berries

Combine berries in a bowl. Top with cereal. Spoon yogurt over berry mixture. Garnish with fresh berries.

Maple Hot Chocolate

Breakfast Berry Parfait

Rachel Anderson, Livermore, CA

Granny's Country Cornbread

My family loves this tasty cornbread for breakfast...with a sausage patty and orange juice.

Makes 8 servings

1-1/4 c. cornmeal
3/4 c. all-purpose flour
5 T. sugar
2 t. baking powder
1/2 t. salt
1 c. buttermilk
1/3 c. oil
1 egg, beaten
1 c. shredded sharp Cheddar cheese
1 c. canned corn, drained
1 T. jalapeño pepper, minced

Mix together cornmeal, flour, sugar, baking powder and salt in a large bowl. Make a well in center; pour in buttermilk, oil and egg. Stir mixture just until ingredients are lightly moistened. Fold in cheese, corn and jalapeño; pour into a greased 8" cast-iron skillet. Bake at 375 degrees for 20 minutes, or until a tester inserted in the center comes out clean. Let cool slightly; cut into 8 wedges.

Granny's Country Cornbread

Barbara Janssen, Park Beach, ILL

Light & Fluffy Pancakes

Everyone loves pancakes, but when time is short, pancakes can keep the cook in the kitchen too long! These fluffy pancakes can be made ahead and frozen. They warm up beautifully and everyone is happy!

Makes 6 to 8 servings

1 c. all-purpose flour
2 T. sugar
2 t. baking powder
1/2 t. salt
1 egg, beaten
1 c. milk
2 T. oil
Garnish: fresh raspberries, whipped
        cream or powdered sugar

Stir together flour, sugar, baking powder and salt. Add egg, milk and oil all at once to flour mixture, stirring until blended but still slightly lumpy. Pour batter onto a hot, lightly greased griddle or heavy skillet, about 1/4 cup each for regular pancakes or one tablespoon for silver dollar pancakes. Cook on both sides until golden, turning when surface is bubbly and edges are slightly dry. Garnish as desired.

Light & Fluffy Pancakes

Jo Ann, Gooseberry Patch

Puffy Pear Pancake

Top each slice of this oven-baked pancake with a sprinkle of powdered sugar...yum!

Serves 4

3 eggs, beaten
1 c. milk
1 t. vanilla extract
1 c. all-purpose flour
3 T. sugar
1/4 t. salt
4 pears, peeled, cored and sliced
1/4 c. brown sugar, packed
1/4 c. lemon juice

In a large bowl, whisk together eggs and milk. Add vanilla, flour, sugar and salt; whisk to combine. Pour batter into a lightly greased large cast-iron skillet. Transfer skillet to oven. Bake, uncovered, at 425 degrees until golden and puffy, about 25 minutes. Meanwhile, combine pears, brown sugar and lemon juice in a bowl; stir well. Pour into a separate skillet or saucepan over medium heat; sauté until pears are golden, about 5 minutes. Remove from heat. To serve, spoon warm pear mixture over pancake; cut into wedges.

Jill Ball, Highland, UT

Hearty Breakfast Quinoa

I'm always looking for hearty, healthy, yummy breakfast ideas. This one is great! My family likes it, and I feel good that they're starting the day right.

Serves 6

1 c. skim milk
1 c. water
1/4 t. salt
1 c. quinoa, uncooked and rinsed
1 t. cinnamon
2 c. blueberries or raspberries, thawed if frozen
1/3 c. chopped toasted walnuts
1 T. unsweetened flaked coconut

In a saucepan over medium heat, stir together milk, water, salt and quinoa. Bring to a boil. Reduce heat to medium-low; cover and cook for 15 minutes, or until quinoa is tender and liquid is absorbed. Remove from heat; let stand, covered, for about 5 minutes. Gently stir in cinnamon and berries. Just before serving, top with walnuts and coconut.

Hearty Breakfast Quinoa

Vickie, Gooseberry Patch

Sweet Potato Cornbread

This rich cornbread is sure to become your family favorite. Baking it in a skillet makes the edges so wonderfully golden. Serve it with honey butter or raspberry jam.

Makes 6 servings

2 c. self-rising cornmeal mix
1/4 c. sugar
1 t. cinnamon
1-1/2 c. milk
1 c. cooked sweet potato, mashed
1/4 c. butter, melted
1 egg, beaten

Whisk together all ingredients just until dry ingredients are moistened. Spoon the batter into a greased 8" cast-iron skillet or pan. Bake at 425 degrees for 30 minutes, or until a toothpick inserted in center comes out clean.

Jo Ann, Gooseberry Patch

Herbed Mushroom Omelets

Use any favorites from your herb garden...rosemary and chives are really good too. The sautéed mushrooms give a golden look to this pretty omelet.

Serves 2

4 to 6 eggs, beaten
1 T. fresh parsley, chopped
1 t. fresh oregano, chopped
1/2 t. fresh thyme, chopped
salt and pepper to taste
2 t. butter, divided
1-1/2 c. sliced mushrooms

Whisk together eggs and seasonings; set aside. Melt one teaspoon butter in a skillet over medium heat. Add mushrooms and sauté until tender; remove from skillet and set aside. Melt 1/2 teaspoon butter in skillet over low heat; pour in half the egg mixture. Stir eggs around in skillet with a spatula to cook evenly. Lift edges to allow uncooked egg to flow underneath. When almost cooked, spoon on half the mushrooms and fold over. Repeat with remaining egg mixture.

Herbed Mushroom Omelets

Larissa Miller, Bradley Beach, NJ

Orange Yogurt Pancakes

These pancakes are easy to make, fluffy and delicious. My cousin shared a version of this recipe with me, and I've modified it a bit. Have some fun... add chopped fruit or nuts to the batter too if you like.

Makes about 8 pancakes

1-1/2 c. whole-wheat flour
1 T. brown sugar, packed
3/4 t. baking powder
2 eggs
1-1/2 c. vanilla yogurt
1/2 c. milk
1/2 c. orange juice
zest of 1 orange

In a large bowl, combine flour, brown sugar and baking powder. In a separate bowl, whisk eggs; stir in remaining ingredients. Add egg mixture to flour mixture. Stir until combined; let stand for several minutes. Pour batter by 1/4 cupfuls onto an oiled griddle over medium-high heat. Cook until small bubbles form around the edges; flip and cook until other side is golden.

Trish Donley, Pinedale, WY

Cheese & Basil Scones

These savory scones are perfect to serve with fried or scrambled eggs for a hearty breakfast.

Makes one dozen

2 c. all-purpose flour
1/4 c. shredded Parmesan or
    Romano cheese
2 t. baking powder
1 t. baking soda
2 T. fresh basil, chopped
1/4 t. pepper
2/3 c. buttermilk
3 T. olive oil
Optional: 1 egg, beaten

In a bowl, combine flour, cheese, baking powder, baking soda, basil and pepper. Add buttermilk and oil; stir just until moistened. Knead gently 3 times on a floured surface. Line baking sheet with parchment paper. On lined baking sheet, pat dough into a rectangle; cut into 12 rectangles. Pull apart slightly. If desired, brush dough with egg to glaze. Bake at 450 degrees for 10 to 12 minutes, until golden. Serve warm or at room temperature.

Cheese & Basil Scones

Lillian Dahlstrom, Ames, IA

Maple-Walnut Muffins

These are super yummy muffins that our entire family loves...and they are gluten free!

Makes 1-1/2 dozen

1 c. buckwheat flour
1 c. tapioca flour
1 t. baking soda
1/4 t. salt
1/2 c. rice bran
2 bananas, mashed
2/3 c. buttermilk
1/2 c. real maple syrup
1/4 c. oil
1 egg, beaten
2/3 c. walnuts

In a large bowl, mix buckwheat flour, tapioca flour, baking soda and salt. Add rice bran and mix well. Make a well in flour mixture. Set aside. In a medium bowl, mix bananas, buttermilk, maple syrup, oil and egg. Slowly pour banana mixture into flour mixture. Stir until just moistened. Fold in walnuts. Fill 18 greased muffin cups 2/3 full. Bake at 350 degrees for about 20 minutes, until a toothpick inserted in the center comes out clean.

Angela Leikem, Silverton, OR

Good Morning Chile Relleno

Serve with fruit salad and sausage links for a spicy breakfast.

Serves 8 to 10

6-oz. pkg. shredded Cheddar cheese
16-oz. pkg. shredded Monterey Jack cheese
2 4-oz. cans chopped green chiles
4 eggs, beaten
1 c. evaporated milk
1/4 c. all-purpose flour
Garnish: cherry tomatoes, fresh parsley

Sprinkle cheeses and chiles together alternately in a greased 13"x9" baking pan. Whisk together eggs, milk and flour in a medium bowl and pour over cheese mixture. Bake, uncovered, at 350 degrees for 30 minutes. Let cool slightly before serving. Garnish as desired.

Maple-Walnut Muffins

Good Morning Chile Relleno

Lori Hurley, Fishers, IN

French Toast Casserole

A really simple way to make French toast for a crowd. Pop it in the fridge the night before, then all you have to do is bake it the next day. Serve with bacon for a great breakfast!

Makes 6 to 8 servings

1 c. brown sugar, packed
1/2 c. butter
2 c. corn syrup
1 loaf French bread, sliced
5 eggs, beaten
1-1/2 c. milk
Garnish: powdered sugar, maple
    syrup

Melt together brown sugar, butter and corn syrup in a saucepan over low heat; pour into a greased 13"x9" baking pan. Arrange bread slices over mixture and set aside. Whisk together eggs and milk; pour over bread, coating all slices. Cover and refrigerate overnight. Uncover and bake at 350 degrees for 30 minutes, or until lightly golden. Sprinkle with powdered sugar; serve with warm syrup.

Kendall Hale, Lynn, MA

Frosty Orange Juice

The orange juice and milk combination in this drink is so refreshing any time of year!

Makes 4 servings

6-oz. container frozen orange juice
    concentrate, partially thawed
1 c. milk
1 c. water
1 t. vanilla extract
1/3 c. sugar
12 ice cubes

Combine all ingredients in a blender container. Cover and blend until frothy.

French Toast Casserole

Frosty Orange Juice

Connie Herek, Bay City, MI

Mini Pumpkin Spice Loaves

This is a perfect bread for a quick fall breakfast.

Makes 12 mini loaves

3/4 c. butter, softened
3 c. sugar
3 eggs
3 c. all-purpose flour
2 t. baking powder
1 t. baking soda
1/2 t. salt
1 t. cinnamon
1 t. ground cloves
1/4 t. nutmeg
1 c. chopped pecans, toasted
3/4 c. golden raisins
2 c. canned pumpkin
1 t. vanilla extract

Beat butter at medium speed with an electric mixer until creamy. Gradually add sugar, beating well. Add eggs, one at a time, beating just until yellow disappears after each addition. Combine flour, baking power, baking soda, salt and spices. Add pecans and raisins, tossing to coat. Add flour mixture to butter mixture alternately with pumpkin, beginning and ending with flour mixture. Stir in vanilla. Spoon batter into 12 greased and floured 5"x3" mini loaf pans. Bake at 325 degrees for 45 minutes, or until a toothpick inserted in center comes out clean. Cool in pans on a wire rack for 10 minutes; remove from pans and let cool completely.

Mary Mayall, Dracut, MA

Breakfast Spinach Quiche

If you want meat in this dish, add chopped ham or crumbled bacon to this delicious crustless quiche.

Serves 6

10-oz. pkg. frozen chopped spinach, thawed and drained
Optional: 1/2 c. onion or mushrooms, chopped
6 eggs, beaten
1/2 c. milk
1 c. shredded Swiss or Cheddar cheese

Spread chopped spinach in a greased 9" pie plate. Sprinkle onion and/or mushrooms on top, if desired. Beat together eggs and milk; stir in cheese. Pour egg mixture evenly over spinach. Bake at 350 degrees for 25 to 35 minutes, until top is golden and a knife tip inserted into center comes out clean. Cool slightly before cutting.

Breakfast Spinach Quiche

Beth Smith, Manchester, MI

Peggy's Granola

We love to pack this hearty granola in small paper sacks to have ready for a take-along breakfast on those super-busy mornings.

Makes 14 cups, serves 28

4 c. quick-cooking oats, uncooked
2 c. crispy rice cereal
2 c. sliced almonds
2 T. cinnamon
1 c. brown sugar, packed
2/3 c. butter
1/2 c. honey
1 c. raisins or chopped dried fruit

Toss oats, cereal, almonds and cinnamon together in a large bowl; set aside. Combine brown sugar, butter and honey in a heavy saucepan over medium-high heat. Boil, stirring occasionally, until butter is melted and brown sugar is dissolved. Pour over oat mixture; stir to coat. Spread evenly on an aluminum foil-lined baking sheet. Bake at 350 degrees for 10 minutes; stir well. Bake for an additional 10 minutes. Remove from oven and cool 5 minutes; transfer to a large bowl. Stir in raisins or fruit and cool completely. Store in airtight containers.

Shirl Parsons, Cape Carteret, NC

Raspberry Cream Smoothies

I have been making these refreshing smoothies for years. They're a delicious treat for any time of day!

Makes 8 servings

3 c. frozen raspberries
1 c. banana, cubed and frozen
2 c. orange juice
2 c. frozen vanilla yogurt
2 c. raspberry yogurt
2 t. vanilla extract

In a blender, combine frozen fruit and remaining ingredients. Process until smooth; stir, if needed. Pour into chilled glasses.

Presentation
This smoothie has such beautifully intense color, so be sure to showcase it in a clear glass or clear cup.

Raspberry Cream Smoothies

Shirl Parsons, Cape Carteret, NC

Banana-Mango Soy Smoothies

These smoothies have a special creaminess about them that comes from the soy milk. If you prefer, however, you can use regular milk and they are just as delicious.

Serves 6

2 c. vanilla or plain soy milk
2 to 3 bananas, sliced and frozen
6 mangoes, pitted, peeled, cubed and frozen
1 T. honey, or to taste

Combine all ingredients in a blender. Blend on high setting until smooth and frothy. Pour into tall glasses.

Diane Axtell, Marble Falls, TX

Blueberry Scones

Good for breakfast or for a treat any time of the day! Your family will love these amazing scones.

Makes 8 scones

2 c. all-purpose flour
2 T. sugar
1 T. baking powder
1/2 t. baking soda
1/4 t. salt

1 T. orange zest
1/2 c. very cold, butter, cut into
    1-inch pieces
1 c. dried blueberries
2/3 c. buttermilk

In a large bowl, combine flour, sugar, baking powder, baking soda and salt. Add orange zest and mix well. Using a pastry blender, cut in butter until mixture is crumbly, resembling small peas. Add dried blueberries and buttermilk, stirring until just moistened. Turn dough out onto a lightly floured surface; knead 5 or 6 times. Pat into an 8-inch circle. Cut into 8 wedges. Place one inch apart on a lightly greased baking sheet. Bake at 400 degrees for about 15 minutes, or until golden. Let cool. Drizzle with Orange Frosting Drizzle.

ORANGE FROSTING DRIZZLE
2 c. powdered sugar
2 T. orange juice
1 T. butter, melted
1 t. orange zest
1/3 c. sugar

Mix all ingredients in a small bowl. until creamy and smooth. Place in a piping tube or a small plastic sandwich bag; cut off corner of bag. Drizzle frosting onto scones.

Blueberry Scones

Rita Morgan, Pueblo, CO

Southwestern Flatbread

Yum...hot fresh-baked bread to enjoy with eggs and bacon! Easy to change up to Italian flavors too, with oregano and Parmesan cheese.

Makes about 15 pieces

2 t. olive oil, divided
11-oz. tube refrigerated crusty
    French loaf
1/2 c. roasted sunflower kernels
1 t. chili powder
1/2 to 1 t. coarse salt

Brush a 15"x10" jelly-roll pan with one teaspoon oil; unroll dough onto pan. Use a floured rolling pin to roll out into a rectangle. Drizzle dough with remaining oil; brush over dough. In a small bowl, combine sunflower kernels and chili powder; mix well and sprinkle mixture over dough. Firmly press kernels into dough; sprinkle with salt. Bake at 375 degrees for 12 to 16 minutes, until golden. Remove flatbread to a wire rack; cool 10 minutes. Tear or cut into pieces.

Sonya Labbe, Quebec, Canada

Ham & Gruyère Egg Cup

This recipe is always on our Sunday brunch table. It is quick, easy and tasty...very pretty too!

Makes one dozen

12 thin slices deli ham
3/4 c. shredded Gruyère cheese
1 doz. eggs
salt and pepper to taste
3/4 c. half-and-half
2 T. grated Parmesan cheese
Garnish: pepper

Spray 12 muffin cups or ramekins with non-stick vegetable spray. Line each muffin cup or ramekin with a slice of ham folded in half. Top each ham slice with one tablespoon Gruyère cheese, an egg cracked into the cup, a sprinkle of salt and pepper, one tablespoon half-and-half and 1/2 teaspoon Parmesan cheese. Place muffin tin or ramekins on a baking sheet. Bake at 450 degrees for 15 minutes, or until eggs are set. If using a muffin tin, allow baked eggs to cool several minutes before removing them from the muffin tin. Cool slightly before serving in ramekins. Sprinkle with pepper.

Ham & Gruyère Egg Cup

Rebekah Spooner, Huntsville, AL

Johnny Appleseed Toast

I'm a teacher, and we make this every fall to celebrate Johnny Appleseed with our little ones in September. It also makes a wonderful fall breakfast for a special occasion.

Makes 4 servings

4 slices cinnamon-raisin bread
1-1/2 T. butter, divided
1 Gala apple, cored and sliced
4 t. honey
1 t. cinnamon

Spread each slice of bread with one teaspoon of butter. Cover each bread slice with an apple slice; drizzle with one teaspoon honey and sprinkle with cinnamon. Place topped bread slices on an ungreased baking sheet. Broil on high for one to 2 minutes, until toasted and golden.

Johnny Appleseed Toast

Recipe and Photo Courtesy of IowaEgg.org

PB & J Oatmeal

This classic oatmeal breakfast just became a show-stopper with the addition of peanut butter and strawberries.

Serves 4

1 c. long-cooking oats, uncooked
2 c. unsweetened vanilla almond
    milk
4 egg whites, beaten
1/2 t. sugar
1/4 c. crunchy or creamy peanut
    butter
8 strawberries, hulled and sliced

In a medium saucepan, combine oats and almond milk. Cook over medium heat for 8 to 10 minutes or until all the liquid has been absorbed. Add egg whites to the oats and stir continuously, one to 2 minutes. (This will keep the egg whites from immediately scrambling.) Stir in sugar. Remove from heat and portion into bowls. Stir in peanut butter and top with strawberries.

PB & J Oatmeal

LaDeana Cooper, Batavia, OH

Farm-Fresh Omelet

As our garden started producing lots of veggies, my kids started making up their own recipes. For once, Mom was the assistant! Here is an all-time favorite that they came up with.
We like our vegetables crisp, but if you prefer them more tender, sauté before adding to the omelet.

Makes one serving

2 eggs
1 T. skim milk
1/2 t. pepper
1/2 t. canola oil
1 t. green onion, thinly sliced
1 T. asparagus, chopped into small pieces
1 T. carrot, cut into thin sticks
2 T. tomato, diced

Beat together eggs, milk and pepper in a bowl; set aside. Spray skillet with non-stick vegetable spray. Pour oil into a skillet over medium heat; add egg mixture. Cook until set underneath; flip gently and cook other side. Top half of omelet with vegetables. Fold over and turn out onto a plate.

Henry Burnley, Ankeny, IA

Potato-Egg Bake

This pretty and tasty egg bake makes a great dish for a special day or holiday brunch. Serve with fresh fruit and hot coffee.

Serves 9

8 eggs
3/4 c. whole milk
2-1/2 c. frozen shredded potatoes
1-1/2 c. shredded Cheddar cheese, divided
1/2 c. fresh spinach, chopped
Optional: 1/2 c. cooked ham, cubed
1 T. green pepper, chopped
1 T. red pepper, chopped
1 t. salt
1 t. fresh chives, chopped
1/2 t. pepper

In a small mixing bowl, beat eggs with a whisk until well blended and frothy. Beat in milk. Set aside. In a large mixing bowl, combine potatoes, 3/4 cup cheese, spinach, ham (if using), green and red sweet pepper, salt, chives and black pepper. Mix well. Add egg mixture to potato mixture and mix well. Pour into a greased shallow 5-cup casserole dish. Sprinkle with remaining cheese. Bake at 325 degrees for about 45 minutes, until mixture is set and knife comes out clean when inserted in the center. Serve immediately.

Potato-Egg Bake

Lisa McClelland, Columbus, OH

Oatmeal Waffles

My mother didn't trust waffle mixes, so this is her made-from-scratch recipe. Yum!

Makes 10 waffles

1-1/2 c. all-purpose flour
1 c. quick-cooking rolled oats, uncooked
1 T. baking powder
1/4 t. sea salt
2 t. pumpkin pie spice
1 t. vanilla extract
2 eggs, lightly beaten
1-1/2 c. skim milk
1/4 c. butter, melted and cooled
2 T. brown sugar, packed
Garnish: fresh raspberries, syrup

In a large bowl, mix together flour, oats, baking powder, salt, spice and vanilla; set aside. In a separate bowl, stir together remaining ingredients except garnish. Add egg mixture to flour mixture; stir until blended. Pour batter by 1/3 cupfuls onto a preheated, lightly greased waffle iron. Bake according to manufacturer's instructions. Serve topped with fresh raspberries and syrup, as desired.

Recipe and Photo Courtesy of IowaEgg.org

Veggie & Cheddar Crustless Quiche

These little nuggets of goodness have everything you need to start your day. Freeze any leftovers in individual portions and heat up for a quick breakfast on a busy day.

Serves 8

8 eggs
3/4 c. milk
1/4 t. salt
1/4 t. pepper
1-1/2 c. shredded Cheddar cheese
1 c. broccoli, chopped
1/2 c. red onion, finely chopped
1/2 c. red pepper, chopped

In a large bowl, whisk together eggs, milk, salt and pepper. Stir in cheese, broccoli, onion and red pepper. Spoon mixture evenly into a greased 6-cup jumbo muffin pan. Bake at 350 degrees for 35 to 40 minutes, until tops are puffed and knife inserted in center of quiche comes out clean. Run knife around edges of muffin cups; carefully remove quiches.

Oatmeal Waffles

Veggie & Cheddar Crustless Quiche

Lizzy Burnley, Ankeny, IA

Lizzy's Make-Ahead Egg Casserole

This recipe is a favorite for breakfast, lunch or dinner! And preparing it ahead makes it that much easier!

Serves 12

1 doz. eggs
1 c. cooked ham, diced
3 c. whole milk
12 frozen waffles
2 c. shredded Cheddar cheese,
    divided

In a large bowl, beat eggs. Stir in ham and milk. Grease a 13"x9" baking pan. Place one layer of waffles in the bottom of the pan. Pour half of the mixture on the waffles. Sprinkle with half of the cheese. Continue layering waffles, egg mixture and cheese. Cover and refrigerate overnight. Uncover and bake at 350 degrees for about one hour or until eggs are set.

Lizzy's Make-Ahead Egg Casserole

Victoria Mitchel, Gettysburg, PA

Mile-High Biscuits

These biscuits are great with just a little butter or jelly, but they are extra good with a dollop of sausage gravy on top!

Makes one dozen

2 c. all-purpose flour
4 t. baking powder
1/4 t. baking soda
3/4 t. salt
5 T. chilled butter, diced
1 c. buttermilk

Combine flour, baking powder, baking soda and salt in a food processor; add butter. Pulse just until mixture resembles coarse crumbs. Transfer mixture to a large bowl; add buttermilk. Stir until mixture begins to hold together. Turn out onto a lightly floured surface. Working quickly, knead until most of the dough sticks together. Pat out dough into a 12" circle, 1/2" thick. Cut with a biscuit cutter, quickly re-gathering dough until about 12 biscuits are cut. Arrange biscuits in a parchment paper-lined 13"x9" baking pan. Set pan on center oven rack. Bake at 450 degrees for about 10 minutes, until lightly golden. Serve warm.

Mile-High Biscuits

Recipe Courtesy of IowaEgg.org

Mini Breakfast Pizza

For some extra spice, top pizzas with red pepper flakes, dried oregano or any other toppings you like.

Serves 4

8-oz. turkey breakfast sausages, casings removed
6 eggs, beaten
1/2 c. pizza sauce
4 6-inch whole-wheat pita breads
1 c. shredded part-skim mozzarella cheese

Coat a large non-stick skillet with non-stick vegetable spray. Cook sausage over medium heat, breaking into crumbles, until browned and cooked through. Drain; return to heat. Pour eggs over sausage in skillet. As eggs begin to set, gently pull the eggs across the pan with a spatula, forming large soft curds. Continue cooking, pulling, lifting and folding eggs until thickened and some visible liquid egg remains. Do not stir constantly. Do not overcook. Spread 2 tablespoons pizza sauce on each pita bread; place on baking sheet(s). Top with eggs and cheese, dividing evenly. Bake at 450 degrees for about 5 minutes, until cheese is melted.

Etha Hutchcroft, Ames, IA

Strawberry Preserves Smoothies

Serve this farm-fresh breakfast smoothie in small canning jars with a pretty straw for a fun presentation.

Makes 4 servings

2 T. strawberry preserves
1 c. crushed pineapple
1 c. orange juice
3 c. fresh strawberries, hulled and sliced
8-oz. container strawberry yogurt
8-oz. container plain yogurt

Combine all ingredients in a blender; process until smooth. Pour into chilled jelly jars to serve.

Strawberry Preserves Smoothies

Nacho Burgers

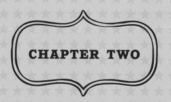

CHAPTER TWO

Time for Lunch

Whether you crave a burger, a freshly tossed salad or a warm bowl of soup, you'll find the perfect recipe for your middle-of-the-day meal in this chapter of lunch favorites.

Apple-Walnut Chicken Salad, Page 99   Garbanzo Bean Soup, Page 122

Teresa Willett, Ontario, Canada

Grilled Chicken & Zucchini Wraps

So easy to make and so yummy to eat, these chicken wraps will be your go-to lunch.

Makes 8 servings

4 boneless, skinless chicken breasts
6 zucchini, sliced lengthwise into
   1/4-inch thick slices
2 T. olive oil
salt and pepper to taste
1/4 c. ranch salad dressing, divided
8 10-inch whole-grain flour tortillas
8 leaves lettuce
1/4 c. shredded low-fat Cheddar
   cheese

Brush chicken and zucchini with olive oil; sprinkle with salt and pepper. Grill chicken over medium-high heat for 5 minutes. Turn chicken over; add zucchini to grill. Grill 5 minutes longer, or until chicken juices run clear and zucchini is tender. Slice chicken into strips; set aside. For each wrap, spread salad dressing on a tortilla. Top with a lettuce leaf, chicken and zucchini. Sprinkle with cheese; roll up.

Wendy Perry, Lorton, VA

Buffalo Chicken Salad Sliders

These quick-to-make sandwiches are perfect when you have a big, hungry crowd!

Makes 8 sandwiches

3/4 c. mayonnaise
1/4 c. sour cream
2 T. hot pepper sauce
1 t. garlic powder
1/2 t. salt
3 c. cooked chicken, diced
3/4 c. celery, diced
1/2 c. sweet onion, diced
8 potato dinner rolls, split

In a bowl, combine mayonnaise, sour cream, hot sauce and seasonings until well mixed. Stir in chicken, celery and onion. Fill sliced rolls with chicken mixture.

Grilled Chicken & Zucchini Wraps

Buffalo Chicken Salad Sliders

Shirl Parsons, Cape Carteret, NC

Mediterranean Sandwiches

The roasted red pepper in this recipe makes these sandwiches extra good.

Makes 12 open-faced sandwiches

4 4-oz. boneless, skinless chicken
　breasts
1 t. dried basil
1/8 t. salt
1/4 t. pepper
1 c. cucumber, chopped
1/4 c. light mayonnaise
1/4 c. roasted red pepper, chopped
1/4 c. sliced black olives
1/4 c. plain Greek yogurt
1/4 t. garlic powder
6 kaiser rolls, split
Garnish: lettuce leaves

Combine chicken, basil, salt and pepper in a stockpot. Cover with water and bring to a boil. Reduce heat and simmer, covered, 10 to 12 minutes until chicken is no longer pink in center. Remove chicken from pan; set aside to cool. Cube chicken and combine with remaining ingredients except rolls and garnish. Toss well to coat. Open rolls and lay lettuce on one side of roll. Add chicken salad mixture.

Amber Sutton, Naches, WA

Cherry Tomato Hummus Wraps

I love those little tomatoes that you can eat like candy straight from the vine! When I added garden-fresh basil and some other salad ingredients I had on hand, I was delightfully surprised with this resulting summer lunch.

Makes 4 servings

1/4 c. hummus
4 8-inch flour tortillas, warmed
1 c. cherry tomatoes, halved
1/2 c. Kalamata olives, chopped
1/3 c. crumbled feta cheese
6 sprigs fresh basil, snipped

Spread one tablespoon hummus down the center of each tortilla. Divide remaining ingredients evenly over hummus. Roll up tortillas and serve.

Cherry Tomato Hummus Wraps

Lori Rosenberg, Cleveland, OH

Spring Ramen Salad

This yummy recipe is truly made to clean out the fridge...you can put almost anything in it!

Makes 4 servings

3-oz. pkg. chicken-flavored
    ramen noodles
1 t. sesame oil
1/2 c. seedless grapes, halved
1/2 c. apple, cored and diced
1/4 c. pineapple, diced
2 green onions, diced
1 c. cooked chicken, cubed
1 c. Muenster cheese, cubed
1-1/2 T. lemon juice
1/8 c. canola oil
1 t. sugar
Garnish: sesame seed

Set aside seasoning packet from ramen noodles. Cook noodles according to package directions. Drain noodles; rinse with cold water. In a bowl, toss sesame oil with noodles to coat. Stir in fruit, onions, chicken and cheese. In a separate bowl, whisk together lemon juice, canola oil, sugar and 1/2 teaspoon of contents of seasoning packet. Pour over noodle mixture; toss to coat. Garnish with sesame seed. Cover and chill before serving.

Charlotte Orm, Florence, AZ

California Avocado Soup

This soup is so pretty and makes a lovely luncheon soup any time of the year.

Serves 6

1/2 c. onion, chopped
1 T. butter
2 14-1/2 oz. cans chicken broth
2 potatoes, peeled and cubed
1/2 t. salt
1/4 t. pepper
2 ripe avocados, halved and pitted
Garnish: sour cream, real bacon bits

In a large saucepan over medium heat, sauté onion in butter until tender. Add broth, potatoes, salt and pepper; bring to a boil. Reduce heat to low. Cover and simmer for 15 to 25 minutes, until potatoes are tender. Remove from heat; cool slightly. Working in batches, scoop avocado pulp into a blender; add potato mixture with broth. Cover and process until puréed. Return to pan; heat through. Garnish with sour cream and bacon bits.

California Avocado Soup

Melody Taynor, Everett, WA

Chilled Apple & Cheese Salad

As a girl, I was convinced that I didn't like gelatin salads. But when my Aunt Clara served this at an anniversary party, I found I had been mistaken!

Makes 6 servings

3-oz. pkg. lemon gelatin mix
1 c. boiling water
3/4 c. cold water
2/3 c. red apple, cored and finely
    chopped
1/3 c. shredded Cheddar cheese
1/4 c. celery, chopped

In a bowl, dissolve gelatin in boiling water. Stir in cold water; chill until partially set. Fold in remaining ingredients. Pour into a 3-cup mold. Cover and chill 3 hours, or until firm. Unmold onto a serving plate.

Good News

Gelatin also comes in a sugar-free variety, so if you are watching your weight or are diabetic, you can still enjoy this salad.

Abby Snay, San Francisco, CA

Chicken Taco Salad

Such a colorful and tasty taco lunch!

Makes 8 servings

8 6-inch flour tortillas
2 c. cooked chicken breast, shredded
2 t. taco seasoning mix
1/2 c. water
2 c. lettuce, shredded
1/2 c. black beans, drained
    and rinsed
1 c. shredded Cheddar cheese
1/2 c. green onion, sliced
1/2 c. canned corn, drained
2-1/4 oz. can sliced black olives,
    drained
1/2 avocado, pitted, peeled and cubed
Garnish: fresh salsa

Microwave tortillas on high setting for one minute, or until softened. Press each tortilla into an ungreased jumbo muffin cup to form a bowl shape. Bake at 350 degrees for 10 minutes; cool. Combine chicken, taco seasoning and water in a skillet over medium heat. Cook, stirring frequently, until blended, about 5 minutes. Divide lettuce among tortilla bowls. Top with chicken and other ingredients, garnishing with salsa.

Chicken Taco Salad

Rachel Ripley, Pittsburgh, PA

Sweet Ambrosia Salad

Kids of all ages love this sweet, creamy salad!

Makes 8 to 10 servings

20-oz. can pineapple chunks, drained
14-1/2 oz. jar maraschino cherries, drained
11-oz. can mandarin oranges, drained
8-oz. container sour cream
10-1/2 oz. pkg. pastel mini marshmallows
1/2 c. sweetened flaked coconut

Combine fruit in a large bowl; stir in sour cream until coated. Fold in marshmallows and coconut; cover and chill overnight.

Larry Bodner, Dublin, OH

Grilled Chicken Salad

The chopped apple in this dressing makes this salad seem extra special and elegant.

Makes 4 servings

1 c. apple, peeled, cored and finely chopped
1/2 c. apple juice
1 T. cider vinegar
1 t. cornstarch
4 boneless, skinless chicken breasts
6-oz. pkg. mixed salad greens
1/2 c. red pepper, sliced
3/4 c. crumbled blue cheese
1/2 c. shredded Cheddar cheese
1/4 c. sliced almonds, toasted

Combine apple, juice, vinegar and cornstarch in a small saucepan over medium heat; cook and stir until thickened. Chill. Grill chicken breasts until juices run clear; let cool, then slice. Divide salad greens among 4 serving plates; top each with grilled chicken, red pepper and a sprinkling of cheeses and almonds. Drizzle with dressing and serve immediately.

Grilled Chicken Salad

Rita Miller, Lincolnwood, IL

Arugula & Nectarine Salad

We love the combination of the spicy arugula and sweet nectarines. The walnuts add the perfect crunch!

Makes 4 servings

1/4 c. balsamic vinegar
1 T. Dijon mustard
1 T. honey
1/4 t. salt
pepper to taste
1/4 c. extra-virgin olive oil
1/4 lb. fresh arugula, torn
2 ripe nectarines, halved, pitted and
  sliced
3/4 c. chopped walnuts
1/2 c. crumbled feta cheese

Combine vinegar, mustard, honey, salt and pepper in a shaker jar. Add oil; shake until blended. Divide arugula among 4 salad plates; arrange nectarine slices over arugula. Sprinkle with walnuts and cheese; drizzle with salad dressing to taste.

Arugula & Nectarine Salad

Larry Anderson, New Orleans, LA

Herbed Zucchini & Bowties

A beautiful dish for a special luncheon!

Serves 4

2 T. butter
1/4 c. oil, divided
1 onion, chopped
1 clove garlic, chopped
1 green pepper, diced
3 zucchini, halved lengthwise and
  sliced
1 t. dried parsley
1 t. dried rosemary, crumbled
1 t. dried basil
16-oz. pkg. bowtie pasta, cooked
1/2 c. shaved Parmesan cheese

In a skillet over medium heat, melt butter with 2 tablespoons oil. Add onion and garlic; sauté for 5 minutes. Stir in green pepper; sauté for an additional 3 minutes. Stir in zucchini and herbs; cover and cook over low heat for 5 to 8 minutes, until zucchini is tender. Add remaining oil; toss with bowties. Sprinkle with Parmesan cheese.

Herbed Zucchini & Bowties

Wendy Ball, Battle Creek, MI

Caesar Focaccia Sandwich

Now that I'm retired after 28 years of federal service, I enjoy being able to try new recipes on my family. This one was a big winner!

Serves 2 to 4

2 c. mixed salad greens
1/4 c. Caesar salad dressing
8-inch round focaccia bread or
    round loaf, halved horizontally
4 slices Cheddar cheese
1/4 lb. deli ham, thinly shaved
1/4 lb. deli turkey, thinly shaved
1 tomato, sliced
1 slice red onion, separated into
    rings
Garnish: pickles, potato chips

Toss salad greens with salad dressing in a small bowl; set aside. Layer the bottom half of focaccia with greens mixture and remaining ingredients except garnish. Add the top half of focaccia; cut into halves or quarters. Serve with pickles and chips on the side.

Lois Carswell, Kennesaw, GA

Confetti Corn & Rice Salad

This colorful salad is a favorite at our family gatherings and barbecues, especially during the summer when we can use fresh-picked sweet corn...yum!

Serves 8

4 ears corn, husked
1-1/2 c. cooked rice
1 red onion, thinly sliced
1 green pepper, halved and thinly
    sliced
1 pt. cherry tomatoes, halved
Optional: 1 jalapeño pepper, thinly
    sliced

Boil or grill ears of corn until tender; let cool. With a sharp knife, cut corn from cob in "planks." In a serving bowl, combine rice, red onion, green pepper, tomatoes and jalapeño pepper, if using. Mix in corn, keeping some corn planks for top. Drizzle with Simple Dressing. Serve at room temperature or refrigerate overnight before serving. Add reserved corn on top.

SIMPLE DRESSING
2 T. red wine vinegar
2 T. olive oil
salt and pepper to taste

Whisk all ingredients together.

Confetti Corn & Rice Salad

Jennifer Weber, Williamsville, NY

Grilled Veggie Combo

My husband and I created this recipe together when we planted our first garden.

Makes 4 servings

1 zucchini, thinly sliced
1 yellow squash, thinly sliced
1 red onion, thinly sliced
1 T. garlic, minced
1 T. olive oil
fresh basil, oregano or parsley to
   taste, chopped

Coat inside of a vegetable grill basket with non-stick vegetable spray; fill with vegetables and garlic. Place on a grill preheated to medium heat. Cover and cook until vegetables are crisp-tender. Remove from grill; transfer vegetables to a serving dish. Lightly drizzle with oil; add desired chopped herbs and serve immediately.

Michelle McFadden-DiNicola,
Highland Park, NJ

Grandma's Pastina

The tiny pasta in this soup makes it so special and fun for the entire family! We looked forward to this lunch with Grandma on the weekends.

Makes 2 to 3 servings

4 c. water
3 cubes chicken bouillon
2 cubes beef bouillon
3/4 c. tiny star or alphabet soup
   pasta, uncooked
1/2 c. fresh parsley, coarsely chopped
1/8 t. pepper
2 eggs
salt and pepper to taste
Optional: grated Parmesan cheese

Place water and bouillon cubes in a soup pot over medium heat. Stir to break up bouillon cubes once the water is simmering. Stir in pasta, parsley and pepper; boil until pasta is tender, 3 to 4 minutes. Turn heat down to lowest possible setting. In a small bowl, whisk eggs lightly with a fork; season with salt and pepper to taste. While stirring the soup, slowly pour in eggs. Continue stirring until eggs begin to turn white. Allow eggs to cook through, about one additional minute. Sprinkle with Parmesan cheese if desired. Serve hot.

Grandma's Pastina

Dana Thompson, Delaware, OH

Quick & Easy Veggie Salad

This is our go-to salad when we are craving veggies but have little prep time. So easy and so good!

Makes 6 servings

1/2 head cauliflower, chopped
3 c. broccoli, chopped
1 tomato, chopped
1/4 red onion, sliced

Combine cauliflower, broccoli, tomato and onion in a serving bowl. Toss with Vinaigrette Dressing.

VINAIGRETTE DRESSING

3 T. lemon juice
1 T. canola oil
2 t. sugar
1 T. grated Parmesan cheese

Whisk all ingredients together.

Bev Fisher, Mesa, AZ

Grilled Havarti Sandwiches

Now that my children are grown, I'm always looking for recipes that call for ingredients they wouldn't eat. This sandwich is so tasty, I wanted another one the next day after I first tried it!

Makes 4 sandwiches

8 slices French bread
2 t. butter, softened and divided
1/4 c. apricot preserves
1/4 lb. Havarti cheese, sliced
1 avocado, halved, pitted and sliced

Spread 4 slices bread on one side with half the butter and all the preserves. Top with cheese, avocado and another slice of bread; spread remaining butter on outside of sandwiches. Heat a large skillet over medium heat. Cook sandwiches for 2 to 3 minutes, until bread is golden and cheese begins to melt. Turn over; press down slightly with a spatula. Cook until golden.

Grilled Havarti Sandwiches

Janice Woods, Northern Cambria, PA

Chilled Melon Soup

This tasty and beautiful recipe is perfect for summer get-togethers with friends.

Makes 4 to 6 servings

3 c. cantaloupe melon, peeled, seeded
  and chopped
2 T. sugar, divided
1/4 c. orange juice, divided
1/8 t. salt, divided
3 c. honeydew melon, peeled, seeded
  and chopped
Garnish: fresh mint sprigs or orange
  slices

In a blender, process cantaloupe, half the sugar, half the juice and half the salt until smooth. Cover and refrigerate. Repeat with honeydew and remaining ingredients except garnish. Refrigerate, covered, in separate containers. To serve, pour equal amounts of each mixture at the same time on opposite sides of individual soup bowls. Garnish as desired.

Lucy Davis, Colorado Springs, CO

Lucy's Sausage Salad

This deliciously different salad may be made ahead and chilled for one to 2 hours, or served immediately. It is so quick to make!

Serves 4

14-oz. pkg. mini smoked beef
  sausages, divided
1 t. canola oil
1 c. corn
15-1/2 oz. can black beans, drained
  and rinsed
1 T. canned jalapeño pepper, seeded
  and minced
1 c. red pepper, chopped
Garnish: fresh cilantro sprigs

Measure out half the sausages; set aside for a future use. Slice remaining sausages into 3 pieces each. In a skillet, sauté sausages in oil over medium heat until lightly golden; drain. In a large bowl, combine corn, beans, jalapeño and red pepper. Stir in sausage. Toss with Dressing; garnish with cilantro.

DRESSING
3 T. plain yogurt
3 T. sour cream
1/4 c. picante sauce
1/2 c. fresh cilantro, chopped
salt and pepper to taste

Whisk together all ingredients.

Lucy's Sausage Salad

Sandra Sullivan, Aurora, CO

Gingered Shrimp & Snow Peas

A flavorful salad that's a meal in itself!

Serves 4

3/4 lb. snow peas, trimmed
1-1/4 lbs. uncooked medium shrimp, cleaned
6 radishes, thinly sliced
4 green onions, thinly sliced
1/3 c. vinegar
1 T. canola oil
1 T. toasted sesame oil
1 T. fresh ginger, peeled and grated
salt to taste
2 T. toasted sesame seeds

Place a steamer basket in a large saucepan; fill pan with water and bring to a boil. Add snow peas; cover and cook 2 minutes. Remove basket, reserving boiling water in saucepan; transfer peas to a bowl of ice water to cool. Drain peas and pat dry; cut on the diagonal into 1/2-inch pieces.

Gingered Shrimp & Snow Peas

Add shrimp directly to boiling water; return to a boil and cook 2 minutes. Drain shrimp; plunge into a bowl of ice water. Drain and pat dry; slice shrimp in half lengthwise. In a large bowl, toss together shrimp, peas, radishes and onions. In a small bowl, whisk together vinegar, oils and ginger; add salt to taste. Drizzle vinegar mixture over salad and top with sesame seeds.

Recipe and Photo Courtesy of IowaEgg.org

Egg Bagel Sandwich

This bagel sandwich makes the perfect lunch, high in protein and full of flavor.

Serves 2

1 t. oil
2 eggs
2 T. garden vegetable cream cheese
2 "everything spice" bagels, halved and toasted
2 slices Pepper Jack cheese
1/2 avocado, pitted and mashed
4 slices tomato
several fresh spinach leaves

Heat oil in a non-stick skillet over medium heat. Break eggs into skillet and cook 3 to 4 minutes, turning once, until eggs are cooked to desired doneness. To assemble sandwich, spread cream cheese on bottom half of bagels. Top with egg, cheese, avocado, spinach and tomato. Serve immediately,

Egg Bagel Sandwich

Tiffani Schulte, Wyandotte, MI

Blue-Ribbon Corn Dog Bake

This casserole is oh-so easy, and it really does taste like a county fair corn dog!

Serves 6

1/3 c. sugar
1 egg, beaten
1 c. all-purpose flour
3/4 T. baking powder
1/2 t. salt
1/2 c. yellow cornmeal
1/2 T. butter, melted
3/4 c. milk
16-oz. pkg. hot dogs, sliced into
   bite-size pieces

In a small bowl, mix together sugar and egg. In a separate bowl, mix together flour, baking powder and salt. Add flour mixture to sugar mixture. Add cornmeal, butter and milk, stirring just to combine. Fold in hot dog pieces. Pour into a well-greased 8"x8" baking pan. Bake, uncovered, at 375 degrees for about 15 minutes, or until a toothpick inserted near the center comes out clean.

Stacie Avner, Delaware, OH

Nacho Burgers

This is just about the best burger you'll every eat! The avocado topping makes it a hit every time. And the chips in the meat mixture adds so much flavor. My kids ask for this burger more than any other!

Serves 5

1 small avocado, pitted, peeled and
   diced
1 plum tomato, diced
2 green onions, chopped
2 t. lime juice
1-1/4 lbs. lean ground beef
1 egg, beaten
3/4 c. nacho-flavored tortilla chips,
   crushed
1/4 c. fresh cilantro, chopped
1/2 t. chili powder
1/2 t. ground cumin
salt and pepper to taste
1-1/4 c. shredded Pepper Jack cheese
5 whole-wheat hamburger buns,
   split

Mix together avocado, tomato, onions and lime juice; mash slightly and set aside. Combine beef, egg, chips and seasonings in a large bowl. Form into 5 patties; grill to desired doneness, turning to cook on both sides. Sprinkle cheese over burgers; grill until melted. Serve on buns; spread with avocado mixture.

Nacho Burgers

Jolene Koval, Ontario, Canada

Jolene's Chickpea Medley

This unusual salad goes together in jiffy! It's terrific for warm-weather meals grilled in the backyard.

Makes 6 servings

15-oz. can garbanzo beans, drained
   and rinsed
1 red pepper, diced
1 c. kale, finely shredded
1 zucchini, chopped
1 ear corn, kernels cut off, or
   1/2 c. frozen corn, thawed
1/4 c. Italian salad dressing

In a salad bowl, combine beans and vegetables. Drizzle with salad dressing; toss to mix. Let stand 15 minutes before serving to allow flavors to blend.

Wendy Jacobs, Idaho Falls, ID

Grilled Veggie Sandwich

Use any of your favorite freshly picked vegetables for this sandwich!

Makes 10 servings

1/4 c. balsamic vinegar
2 T. olive oil
1 T. fresh basil, chopped
1 t. molasses
1-1/2 t. fresh thyme, chopped
1/4 t. pepper
3 zucchini, sliced
1/2 yellow pepper, coarsely chopped
2 red peppers, coarsely chopped
1 onion, sliced
16-oz. loaf whole-grain French-style
   bread, halved horizontally
3/4 c. crumbled feta cheese
2 T. light mayonnaise
1/4 c. freshly grated Parmesan
   cheese

Whisk together vinegar, olive oil, basil, molasses, thyme, and pepper. Place zucchini, peppers and onion in a large plastic zipping bag. Add vinegar mixture; seal and refrigerate 2 hours, turning bag occasionally. Remove vegetables from bag and set aside; reserve marinade. Brush 3 or 4 tablespoons reserved marinade over cut sides of bread. Lightly coat grill pan with non-stick vegetable spray; add vegetables and grill 5 minutes, basting occasionally with remaining marinade. Turn vegetables, baste and grill 2 more minutes. Place bread, cut-sides down on grill and grill 3 minutes or until bread is toasted. Combine feta cheese and mayonnaise; spread evenly over cut sides of bread. Layer grilled vegetables on bread; add Parmesan cheese. Slice into 10 sections.

Grilled Veggie Sandwich

Jo Cline, Smithville, MO

Sausage Bean Gumbo

Quick & easy...ready in 30 minutes!

Serves 8

14-oz. smoked pork sausage link, sliced
3 15-1/2 oz. cans Great Northern beans
14-1/2 oz. can diced tomatoes with sweet onions
1 stalk celery, diced
1/2 c. green pepper, diced
1/2 t. garlic powder
1/4 t. pepper
Garnish: fresh cilantro, chopped

In a large saucepan over low heat, combine all ingredients except garnish. Do not drain cans. Cover and simmer about 30 minutes, stirring occasionally. Sprinkle servings with cilantro, if desired.

Sausage Bean Gumbo

Cherylann Smith, Efland, NC

Herbed Sausage Quiche

This quiche is as beautiful as it is delicious! Serve for a fancy luncheon with fresh fruit and hot tea.

Serves 8

9-inch frozen pie crust, thawed
1 c. ground pork breakfast sausage, browned and drained
3 eggs, beaten
1 c. whipping cream
1 c. shredded Cheddar cheese
1 sprig fresh rosemary, chopped
1-1/2 t. Italian seasoning
1/4 t. salt
1/4 t. pepper
Garnish: fresh rosemary sprig

Bake pie crust according to package directions. In a bowl, mix together remaining ingredients except garnish; spread into crust. Bake, uncovered, at 450 degrees for about 15 minutes. Reduce heat to 350 degrees, cover with aluminum foil and bake for 10 more minutes or until set. Garnish with rosemary sprig. Cut into wedges to serve.

Herbed Sausage Quiche

Jo Ann, Gooseberry Patch

Stewed Lentils with Tomatoes

A satisfying side dish that's packed with good-for-you ingredients.

Makes 8 servings

2 t. olive oil
2 c. yellow onions, diced
2 c. carrots, peeled and diced
3 cloves garlic, minced
28-oz. can whole plum tomatoes
1 c. dried French green lentils, uncooked
3 c. low-sodium chicken or vegetable broth
2 t. fresh thyme, chopped
2 t. curry powder
1/4 t. pepper
1/4 t. salt
1 T. red wine vinegar

Heat oil in a large saucepan over medium-low heat; add onions and carrots. Cook, stirring occasionally, for 8 to 10 minutes, until onions are lightly golden. Add garlic; cook for another minute. Meanwhile, pour tomatoes and their juice into a blender. Process until coarsely chopped; pour into onion mixture along with lentils, broth, thyme, curry powder and pepper. Bring to a boil. Reduce heat to low; cover and simmer for about 40 minutes, until lentils are tender. Remove from heat; cover and let stand for 10 minutes. At serving time, stir in salt and vinegar.

Becky Butler, Keller, TX

Apple-Walnut Chicken Salad

This tasty recipe uses the convenience of a roast chicken from your grocery store's deli...what a great time-saver!

Makes 6 servings

6 c. mixed field greens or baby greens
2 c. deli roast chicken, shredded
1/3 c. crumbled blue cheese
1/4 c. chopped walnuts, toasted
1 Fuji or Gala apple, cored and sliced

In a large salad bowl, toss together all ingredients. Drizzle Balsamic Apple Vinaigrette over salad, tossing gently to coat. Serve immediately.

BALSAMIC APPLE VINAIGRETTE
2 T. frozen apple juice concentrate
1 T. cider vinegar
1 T. white balsamic vinegar
1 t. Dijon mustard
1/4 t. garlic powder
1/3 c. olive oil

Whisk together all ingredients in a small bowl.

Apple-Walnut Chicken Salad

Linda Henderson, Sunset, NC

Roquefort Cut-Out Crackers

These crackers go well with any lunch salad.

Makes 2 dozen

1 c. all-purpose flour
7 T. crumbled Roquefort or blue
    cheese
1 egg yolk
4 t. whipping cream
7 T. butter, softened
1/8 t. salt
cayenne pepper to taste
1/2 t. dried parsley

Stir together all ingredients in a large bowl until dough forms. Cover; let stand for 30 minutes. On a floured surface, roll out dough to 1/8-inch thickness. Cut out dough with a round cookie cutter or other desired shape; arrange on an ungreased baking sheet. Bake at 400 degrees for 7 to 9 minutes, just until golden. Let cool on baking sheet; store in an airtight container.

Gretchen Ham, Pine City, NY

Quick & Easy Tomato Soup

Fresh basil really makes this soup special. The flavors get even better when it is warmed up the next day!

Makes 10 servings

1/2 c. butter, sliced
1 c. fresh basil, chopped
2 28-oz. cans crushed tomatoes
2 cloves garlic, minced
1 qt. half-and-half
salt and pepper to taste
Garnish: fresh parsley, sliced cherry
    tomatoes, croutons

In a large saucepan, melt butter over medium heat. Add basil; sauté for 2 minutes. Add tomatoes with juice and garlic; reduce heat and simmer for 20 minutes. Remove from heat; let cool slightly. Working in batches, transfer tomato mixture to a blender and purée. Strain into a separate saucepan and add half-and-half, mixing very well. Reheat soup over medium-low heat; add salt and pepper to taste. Garnish as desired.

Quick & Easy Tomato Soup

**Recipe and Photo Courtesy of
IowaEgg.org**

Monte Cristo Denver

This recipe may take a little extra time to make, but it is worth the effort. Make if for lunch guests on a special occasion and they will be talking about it for weeks to come!

Serves 2

1/4 lb. pancetta, diced
2 T. red pepper, minced
2 T. jalapeño pepper, minced
1/4 c. green onions, finely chopped
7 eggs, divided
1/2 t. pepper
2 T. mayonnaise
1 T. horseradish mustard
1 T. red raspberry preserves
4 slices bread, crusts removed,
   trimmed to 4 inch squares
4 slices Swiss cheese
1-1/2 c. cornflake cereal, crushed
butter for frying

In a large heavy skillet, over medium heat, cook the pancetta until slightly crisped and fat has rendered. Remove pancetta and set aside, reserving drippings in skillet. Whisk the pancetta, peppers, green onions, 4 eggs and pepper together. Pour into skillet. Cook over medium heat until set and slightly puffed, turning once. Remove from skillet and set aside. Trim to two 4-inch squares.
In a small bowl, whisk together mayonnaise, mustard and preserves. Spread one side of each slice of bread with this mixture. Top one bread slice with one cheese slice, one egg square, another cheese slice and a second slice of bread, mayonnaise-side down. Repeat for second sandwich. Repeat for second sandwich. Cut each sandwich corner to corner, making 4 triangles. Place 3 remaining beaten eggs in a shallow bowl. Place crushed cereal in a separate shallow bowl. Melt a thin layer of butter in the skillet. Dip all sides of each triangle in the beaten eggs, then in the crushed cereal. Cook over medium heat until all sides are golden.

Monte Cristo Denver

Alice Livermore, Rochester, NY

Cream of Asparagus Soup

I love to make this with fresh asparagus from the farmer's market.

Makes 6 to 8 servings

4 c. chicken broth
pepper to taste
1 to 1-1/2 lbs. fresh asparagus, trimmed and broken into 1-inch pieces
1 onion, chopped
1/4 c. butter, sliced
4 c. half-and-half and/or milk
8-oz. pkg. American cheese, diced, or shredded Cheddar cheese
Optional: celery seed to taste

In a soup pot, bring chicken broth and pepper to a boil. Add asparagus and onion; reduce heat to medium-low. Cover and simmer until asparagus is very tender and falling apart. Add butter; stir until melted. Working in batches, process broth mixture in a blender. If a smoother texture is desired, strain broth mixture through a colander into another soup pot; press asparagus pulp through the colander. Return mixture to soup pot. Add half-and-half or milk, cheese and celery seed, if using. Cook and stir over medium-low heat until cheese is melted. Soup keeps well for several days in the refrigerator.

Vickie, Gooseberry Patch

Pepper Steak Sammie

Everyone loves a steak sandwich and this one won't disappoint...enjoy!

Makes 4 sandwiches

1 to 1-1/4 lbs. beef sirloin or ribeye steak
2 green peppers, thinly sliced
1 onion, sliced
1 T. oil
salt and pepper to taste
1/4 c. garlic butter, softened
4 French rolls, split and toasted

Grill or broil steak to desired doneness; set aside. Sauté green peppers and onion in hot oil in a skillet over medium heat until crisp-tender; drain. Slice steak thinly; add to skillet and heat through. Sprinkle with salt and pepper. Spread butter over cut sides of rolls. Spoon steak mixture onto bottom halves of rolls; cover with tops.

Pepper Steak Sammie

Irene Whatling, West Des Moines, IA

Colorful Fruit Soup

This soup is so refreshing! My daughter requests it every spring. Freshly ground black pepper complements the sweet fruit wonderfully.

Makes 6 servings

1 c. seedless grapes, halved
1 c. blueberries
1/2 c. strawberries, hulled and diced
1/2 c. pineapple, peeled and diced
1/2 c. kiwi, peeled and diced
1 c. unsweetened apple juice
1/2 c. orange juice
1/4 t. pepper

Combine fruit in a large bowl. In a measuring cup, mix juices and pepper; pour over fruit mixture. Stir gently. Cover and refrigerate until serving time.

Recipe and Photo Courtesy of IowaEgg.org

Mexican Coffee Cup Scramble

This quick microwave lunch is perfect when you are working at home and don't want to take time for a big lunch, but want a real treat for yourself. Add a side of fresh fruit and your lunch is complete.

Makes 2 servings

2 eggs, beaten
1/2 T. milk
1/4 c. black or pinto beans, drained
    and rinsed
1/4 c. green peppers or green onions,
    chopped
1/4 c. shredded Co-Jack cheese
salt and pepper to taste
Garnish: salsa

Coat a microwave-safe 12-ounce coffee mug with non-stick vegetable spray. Add eggs and milk; beat until blended. Add beans and green pepper or onions. Microwave on high until eggs are almost set, 30 to 45 seconds longer. Season with salt and pepper. Top with cheese and salsa.

Colorful Fruit Soup

Mexican Coffee Cup Scramble

Jackie Crough, Salina, KS

Carrot-Raisin Salad

Grandma made this salad often. It's always very good!

Makes 6 servings

3 c. carrots, peeled and shredded
3/4 c. raisins
1/4 c. chopped walnuts
1/3 c. light mayonnaise

Mix together all ingredients in a large bowl. Serve immediately or cover and refrigerate overnight.

Elijah Dahlstrom, Ames, IA

Quinoa Tabbouleh

Tabbouleh is usually made with couscous, but you'll love this version made using quinoa. You get more protein and the dish is gluten-free.

Serves 4

3/4 c. quinoa, uncooked
1-1/2 c. chicken broth
3/4 c. cucumber, chopped
1/2 c. fresh parsley, snipped
1/4 c. green onions, thinly sliced
1 T. fresh mint, snipped
3/4 c. tomato, chopped
4 lettuce leaves

Place quinoa in a colander and rinse with warm water for 2 minutes. **Note:** quinoa must be rinsed very well to remove the bitterness on the grain. In a saucepan, combine quinoa and chicken broth. Bring to a boil and let cook until quinoa splits and absorbs most of the chicken broth, about 15 minutes. Drain and cool. In a large bowl, combine quinoa, cucumber, parsley, green onions and mint. Drizzle with Tabbouleh Dressing and toss to coat. Cover and chill for 4 to 24 hours. Stir tomato into quinoa mixture just before serving. Serve on lettuce leaves.

TABBOULEH DRESSING

3 T. canola oil
3 T. lemon juice
2 T. water
1 t. Dijon mustard
1/4 t. salt

In a screw-top jar, combine all ingredients. Cover and shake well.

Quinoa Tabbouleh

Dee Ann Ice, Delaware, OH

Delicious BBQ Hamburgers

If you don't want to get out the grill but are hungry for a burger, these hamburgers are perfect for you!

Serves 4 to 6

1 lb. ground beef
1/2 c. milk
1/2 c. soft bread crumbs
1/4 t. pepper
1/4 t. garlic powder
1/2 c. onion, chopped
1/2 c. green pepper, chopped
1 c. catsup
2 t. vinegar
2 t. mustard
1/2 c. sugar
3/4 t. salt

Combine beef, milk, bread crumbs, pepper, garlic powder, onion and green pepper; mix well. Shape into patties and place in a skillet; brown both sides. Place in a greased 13"x9" baking pan; set aside. Combine catsup and remaining ingredients in a mixing bowl; pour over patties. Bake at 350 degrees for one hour.

Recipe and Photo Courtesy of IowaEgg.org

Crustless Spinach Quiche

This quiche makes a perfect light lunch. Serve with a fresh green salad and you'll have a healthy, yummy lunch.

Serves 6

1 T. canola oil
1 onion, chopped
10-oz. pkg. chopped frozen spinach, thawed
6 eggs, beaten
2 c. shredded mozzarella cheese
1 c. shredded sharp Cheddar cheese
1/2 to 1 t. garlic powder
1/4 t. salt
1/8 t. pepper
1/8 t. cayenne pepper
1 tomato, thinly sliced

Heat oil in a large skillet over medium-high heat. Add onion and cook, stirring occasionally, until onion is soft. Stir in spinach and continue cooking until excess moisture has evaporated. Combine eggs, cheese, garlic powder, salt, pepper and cayenne pepper in a large bowl. Add spinach mixture and stir to blend. Spray a 9" pie plate with non-stick vegetable spray and pour mixture into pan. Top with tomato slices. Bake at 350 degrees for 25 to 30 minutes, until eggs are set and knife inserted in the center comes out clean. Let cool for 10 minutes before serving. Cut into 6 slices.

Crustless Spinach Quiche

Laurel Perry, Grayson, GA

Santa Fe Vegetable Salad

A veggie salad with a sassy dressing!

Serves 4 to 6

1 zucchini, diced
1/2 c. canned corn, drained
5 green onions, chopped
1 red pepper, chopped
1 jicama, peeled and diced
1/3 c. chunky salsa, drained
1/3 c. fresh cilantro, chopped
salt and pepper to taste

Combine all ingredients in a serving bowl; toss with Dressing.

DRESSING
1/3 c. lime juice
2 t. hot pepper jelly
1 T. water
1 T. olive oil

Mix together all ingredients in a saucepan; heat over medium heat until jelly melts. Stir well.

Marilyn Epley, Stillwater, OK

Honeyed Fruit & Rice

Jasmine rice is also known as fragrant rice and can be found in many markets or specialty stores.

Makes 2 servings

2 c. cooked jasmine rice
1/3 c. dried cranberries
1/3 c. dried apricots, chopped
1/4 c. honey
Garnish: milk

Stir together hot cooked rice, cranberries, apricots and honey. Divide into 2 bowls; top with milk.

Diane Long, Delaware, OH

Tomato Sandwiches

Use garden tomatoes warm from the summer sun to make these sandwiches extra special.

Makes 5 servings

10 slices pumpernickel bread
3 tomatoes, thickly sliced
10 sprigs fresh watercress
1 red onion, sliced
1 green pepper, sliced
1/4 t. pepper
1 T. mayonnaise

Top each of 5 bread slices with tomato slices, 2 sprigs of watercress, a slice of onion and 2 slices of green pepper. Sprinkle with salt and pepper. Spread mayonnaise over remaining bread slices and top sandwiches.

Tomato Sandwiches

Sandy Westendorp, Grand Rapids, MI

Pumpkin Chowder

This blend of everyday ingredients is anything but ordinary!

Serves 6

1/2 lb. bacon, diced
2 c. onion, chopped
2 t. curry powder
2 T. all-purpose flour
1-lb. pie pumpkin, peeled, seeded
    and chopped
2 potatoes, peeled and cubed
4 c. chicken broth
1 c. half-and-half
salt and pepper to taste
Garnish: toasted pumpkin seeds,
    sliced green onions

Brown bacon in a stockpot over medium heat for 5 minutes; add onion. Sauté for 10 minutes; add curry powder and flour, stirring until smooth and creamy, about 5 minutes. Add pumpkin, potatoes and broth; simmer until pumpkin and potatoes are tender, about 15 minutes. Pour in half-and-half; season with salt and pepper. Simmer for 5 minutes; do not boil. Spoon into soup bowls; garnish with pumpkin seeds and green onions.

Bev Fisher, Mesa, AZ

Tomato Salad with Grilled Bread

Everyone is surprised to see the unique ingredients in this salad. Who would have thought that watermelon, olives and tomatoes would be such a great combination?

Makes 8 servings

3 lbs. tomatoes, cut into chunks
1 cucumber, peeled and sliced
4-oz. container crumbled feta cheese
1/4 c. balsamic vinegar
1/4 t. salt
1/4 t. pepper
8 thick slices crusty wheat bread,
    cubed
2 c. watermelon, cut into 1/2-inch
    cubes
1 red onion, very thinly sliced and
    separated into rings
3.8-oz. can sliced black olives,
    drained
1/4 c. olive oil
1/2 c. fresh basil, torn

In a large serving bowl, combine tomatoes, cucumber, cheese, vinegar, salt and pepper. Toss to mix; cover and chill. Place bread cubes on an ungreased baking sheet. Bake at 350 degrees for 5 minutes, or until lightly golden. At serving time, combine tomato mixture with bread cubes and remaining ingredients. Toss very lightly and serve immediately.

Tomato Salad with Grilled Bread

Sister Toni Spencer, Watertown, SD

Sunflower Strawberry Salad

A great chilled salad for a spring lunch...it is great for Easter and Mother's Day buffets too.

Makes 6 servings

2 c. strawberries, hulled and sliced
1 apple, cored and diced
1 c. seedless green grapes, halved
1/2 c. celery, thinly sliced
1/4 c. raisins
1/2 c. strawberry yogurt
2 T. sunflower kernels
Optional: lettuce leaves

In a large bowl, combine fruit, celery and raisins. Stir in yogurt. Cover and chill one hour. Sprinkle with sunflower kernels just before serving. Spoon over lettuce leaves, if desired.

Evelyn Moriarty, Philadelphia, PA

Vegetable Quinoa Patties

This recipe is my own, adapted from one I found online and tweaked. It has become a family favorite, especially in summertime when fresh-picked veggies are available.

Makes 6 servings

3 eggs
1/2 c. shredded part-skim
    mozzarella cheese
1/2 c. cottage cheese
1/4 c. whole-wheat flour
1 carrot, peeled and grated
1 zucchini, grated
3 T. green, red or yellow pepper,
    grated
3 green onions, finely chopped
1/2 t. ground cumin
1/4 t. garlic powder
1/8 t. salt
1/4 t. pepper
2 c. cooked quinoa
1 T. olive oil

Beat eggs in a large bowl; stir in cheeses and flour, blending well. Mix in vegetables. Combine seasonings; sprinkle over vegetable mixture and mix well. Add cooked quinoa; stir together well. Heat olive oil in a skillet over medium heat. With a small ladle, drop mixture into skillet, making 6 patties. Flatten lightly with ladle to about 1/4-inch thick. Fry patties for 4 to 5 minutes per side, until golden. Serve each serving with 3 tablespoons Dilled Yogurt Dressing.

DILLED YOGURT DRESSING
1/2 c. plain Greek yogurt
1 cucumber, peeled and diced
3 sprigs fresh dill, snipped, or
    1/2 t. dill weed

Stir together all ingredients in a small bowl.

Vegetable Quinoa Patties

Sally Bourdlaies, Bay City, MI

Reuben Tossed Salad

This salad was always a big hit at our son's scouting banquets.

Serves 6 to 8

27-oz. can sauerkraut, drained and
    rinsed
1 c. carrots, peeled and grated
1 c. green pepper, chopped
8-oz. pkg. sliced Swiss cheese, cut
    into thin strips
8-oz. pkg. deli corned beef, thinly
    sliced and cut into thin strips
2 slices rye bread, toasted, buttered
    and cubed

In a large bowl, mix together all ingredients; toss with Dressing.

DRESSING
1/2 c. mayonnaise
2 t. chili sauce
1 T. milk
onion to taste, chopped

Combine all ingredients in a small bowl; mix well.

Irene Whatling, West Des Moines, IA

Peanut Butter Apple-Bacon Sandwich

My family loves this grilled sandwich. I make it for lunch once a week! Sometimes I add some mild Cheddar cheese instead of the peanut butter.

Makes 4 sandwiches

8 slices applewood smoked bacon
8 slices whole-grain bread
1/4 c. peach preserves
1 to 2 apples, cored and thinly sliced
1/4 c. creamy peanut butter
2 to 3 T. butter, softened and divided

In a skillet over medium heat, cook bacon until crisp; drain bacon on paper towels. Spread 4 slices of bread with preserves; layer apple and bacon slices over preserves. Spread remaining bread slices with peanut butter; close sandwiches. Spread tops of sandwiches with half of butter. Place sandwiches butter-side down on a griddle over medium heat. Spread remaining butter on unbuttered side of sandwiches. Cook 2 to 3 minutes per side, until bread is toasted and sandwiches are heated through. Serve warm.

Reuben Tossed Salad

Peanut Butter Apple-Bacon Sandwich

Corinne Gross, Tigard, OR

Grandma's Tomato Muffins

These savory muffins go great with almost any soup and take just a few minutes to make!

Makes one dozen

1 c. all-purpose flour
1 c. whole-wheat flour
1/4 c. grated Parmesan cheese
2 T. sugar
1 T. baking powder
1/4 t. salt
1/2 t. dried oregano
1 egg, beaten
1 c. buttermilk
1/3 c. butter, melted
1 ripe tomato, coarsely chopped
3 T. shredded Parmesan cheese

In a bowl, combine flours, cheese, sugar, baking powder, salt and oregano. Mix well. Stir in egg, buttermilk and butter just until blended. Fold in tomato. Spoon batter into 12 paper-lined muffin cups, filling 3/4 full. Sprinkle with cheese. Bake at 400 degrees for about 15 minutes.

Ardith Field, Goldfield, IA

Greek Salad

So fresh and satisfying, this is my favorite salad to have for lunch.

Serves 10

3-1/2 lbs. romaine lettuce, torn into bite-size pieces
6 roma tomatoes, diced
2 cucumbers, peeled and sliced
3/4 c. whole black olives
1/2 red onion, sliced into rings
1/2 c. crumbled feta cheese
Optional: additional crumbled feta cheese

Place lettuce in a large bowl. Add tomatoes, cucumbers, olives, onion and feta cheese. Toss lightly to mix all ingredients. Drizzle with Greek Vinaigrette Dressing and toss to serve. If desired, top with more feta cheese.

GREEK VINAGRETTE DRESSING

1 clove garlic, minced
3/4 c. red wine vinegar
1/3 c. water
2 T. sugar
2 T. dried basil
2 T. dried oregano
2 T. Dijon mustard
1 c. canola oil

In a medium bowl, combine all ingredients except oil. Mix well. Gradually pour in canola oil while beating with a wire whisk. Refrigerate until ready to serve.

Greek Salad

Audrey Lett, Newark, DE

Suzanne's Tomato Melt

I love this as a quick dinner with a fresh salad...it is so easy to make!

Makes one serving

1/4 c. shredded Cheddar cheese
1 onion bagel or English muffin, split
2 tomato slices
1 T. grated Parmesan cheese
Garnish: fresh basil leaves

Sprinkle half the Cheddar cheese over each bagel or English muffin half. Top with a tomato slice. Sprinkle half the Parmesan cheese over each tomato. Add fresh basil leaf on top. Broil about 6 inches from heat for 4 to 5 minutes, until cheese is bubbly.

Miriam Schultz, Waukee, IA

Garbanzo Bean Soup

This hearty soup makes a perfect vegetarian lunch that is sure to satisfy.

Serves 8

2 T. olive oil
1/2 c. onion, chopped
14-1/2 oz. can petite diced tomatoes, or 1-1/2 c. fresh tomatoes, diced
2 c. chicken broth
15.8-oz. can garbanzo beans, drained and rinsed
2 T. fresh basil, chopped
8-oz. pkg. elbow macaroni, uncooked
Garnish: shredded Parmesan cheese

In a large saucepan, heat olive oil over medium heat. Add onion and cook until tender. Add tomatoes with juice and cook for 5 minutes, stirring occasionally. Add chicken broth, garbanzo beans and basil. Bring to boiling; reduce heat. Simmer covered, for 5 minutes. Meanwhile, cook macaroni as directed on package. Drain well. Add to tomato mixture and stir to combine. Ladle soup into bowls. Top with Parmesan cheese.

Garbanzo Bean Soup

Taffy Apple Pizza

CHAPTER THREE

Coffee-Time Treats

Whether you like a cup of hot coffee, a spot of tea, or a cozy mug of cocoa, coffee-break time just got better with a sweet treat to eat and some good conversation.

Mocha Coffee, Page 140

Chocolate Pinwheels, Page 132

Noah Burnley, Ankeny, IA

Easy Banana Bread

This recipe is a staple at our house!

Makes 10 servings

3 ripe bananas, peeled
1 c. sugar
1/2 c. butter, softened
2 eggs
3 T. buttermilk
1 t. baking powder
1 t. baking soda
1/2 t. salt
2 c. all-purpose flour

Using a fork, mash the bananas until softened. Set aside. In a large mixing bowl, combine sugar and butter. Beat until creamy. Add eggs and mashed bananas; mix well. In a small bowl, mix flour, buttermilk, baking powder, baking soda and salt. Add to butter mixture and mix well. Add flour mixture to butter mixture and mix well. Pour into a greased 9"x5" loaf pan. Bake at 350 degrees for about 40 minutes, or when a toothpick comes out clean when inserted in the center.

Easy Banana Bread

Carol Lytle, Columbus, OH

Blackberry Buckle

We love this blackberry, coffee-cake style treat. Substitute blueberries if you like, for an equally yummy buckle.

Makes 9 servings

2 c. all-purpose flour
2-1/2 t. baking powder
1/4 t. salt
1/2 c. butter
3/4 c. sugar
1 egg, beaten
1/2 c. milk
2 c. blackberries

Stir together flour, baking powder and salt; set aside. In a separate bowl, blend butter and sugar until light and fluffy. Add egg and beat well. Add flour mixture and milk alternately to egg mixture, beating until smooth. Pour into a greased 9"x9" baking pan; top with blackberries and Crumb Topping. Bake at 350 degrees for 50 to 60 minutes, until golden. Serve warm.

CRUMB TOPPING
1/2 c. all-purpose flour
1/2 c. sugar
1/2 t. cinnamon
1/4 c. butter

Sift together flour, sugar and cinnamon. Cut in butter until mixture resembles coarse crumbs.

Blackberry Buckle

Eleanor Dionne, Beverly, MA

Apple & Walnut Scones

These scones are wonderful fresh
from the oven with hot tea or coffee.
They can also be reheated. Wrap
in aluminum foil and place in a
preheated 375-degree oven for
5 minutes, then fold back the foil
and heat for 3 to 4 more minutes.

Makes 8 scones

2-1/4 c. all-purpose flour
1/2 c. sugar
2 t. baking powder
1/2 t. salt
1/2 c. butter
2 eggs, beaten
1/4 c. milk
2 t. vanilla extract
1 t. lemon zest
1 c. cooking apple, peeled, cored and
   chopped
1/2 c. chopped walnuts
1/2 c. light brown sugar, packed
1 t. cinnamon

In a large bowl, combine flour, sugar,
baking powder and salt; mix well.
Cut in butter with 2 knives until
crumbly; set aside. In a small bowl,
mix eggs, milk, vanilla and lemon
zest. Stir into flour mixture; dough
will be sticky. Stir in apples. Grease
an 11-inch circle on a baking sheet.
Place dough on baking sheet; pat into
a 9-inch circle. In a small bowl, mix
nuts, brown sugar and cinnamon;
sprinkle over top. Cut dough into
8 wedges. Bake at 375 degrees for
30 to 35 minutes, until lightly golden.

Dobie Hill, Lubbock, TX

Buttermilk Cinnamon Rolls

These no-yeast cinnamon rolls are
quick to make and disappear
fast! Make plenty to share for
when the neighbors come over
for mid-morning coffee.

Makes 15 rolls

3 c. all-purpose flour
4 t. baking powder
1/4 t. baking soda
1 t. salt
1/2 c. cold butter
1-1/2 c. buttermilk
1/4 c. butter, softened
1/2 c. sugar
1 t. cinnamon

In a large bowl, combine flour, baking
powder, baking soda and salt; cut in
cold butter until crumbs form. Stir in
buttermilk until well blended; knead
dough on a lightly floured surface
for about 4 to 5 minutes. Roll out to
1/4-inch thickness; spread softened
butter over dough to edges. In a small
bowl, mix sugar and cinnamon;
sprinkle over dough. Roll up jelly-roll
style; cut into 1/2-inch slices. Place
on 2 greased baking sheets; bake at
400 degrees for 10 to 12 minutes.

Buttermilk Cinnamon Rolls

COFFEE-TIME TREATS

Michelle Case, Yardley, PA

Break-of-Day Berry Parfait

So pretty served in a parfait or champagne glass for a mid-morning snack.

Serves 2

1 c. strawberries, hulled and sliced
1/2 c. raspberries
1/4 c. blackberries
1 c. bran & raisin cereal
6-oz. container strawberry yogurt

In a bowl, combine berries; divide into 2 small bowls. Top each with cereal. Spoon yogurt over top.

Phyllis Cowgill, La Porte, IN

Granny's Apple Coffee Cake

I remember my dear mother and great-grandmother making this cake with apples and butternuts picked right off the tree and fresh milk from our cows. It's good on a cold brisk morning with a cup of coffee.

Makes 16 servings

1-1/2 c. all-purpose flour
3/4 c. sugar
2 t. baking powder
1 t. cinnamon
1/4 t. salt
1/2 c. butter, softened
2 eggs, beaten
3/4 c. milk
2-1/4 c. apples, peeled, cored, sliced and divided

Combine flour, sugar, baking powder, cinnamon and salt in a bowl; mix well. Blend in butter, eggs and milk; pour half of batter into a greased and floured 9"x9" baking pan. Arrange half of apples over batter; sprinkle with half of the Topping. Arrange remaining apples over Topping, followed by remaining batter and remaining Topping. Bake at 350 degrees for 40 minutes.

TOPPING
1/2 c. brown sugar, packed
3 T. all-purpose flour
1/2 c. chopped walnuts
1-1/2 t. cinnamon
1 T. butter

Combine all ingredients in a bowl; mix well.

Granny's Apple Coffee Cake

COFFEE-TIME TREATS

Loni Ventura, Wimauma, FL

Warm Spiced Milk

This is a tummy-warming beverage... it's like a baked apple in a mug.

Serves 4

2-1/2 c. milk
1/3 c. apple butter
2-1/2 T. maple syrup
1/4 t. cinnamon
1/8 t. ground cloves

Whisk together all ingredients in a heavy saucepan over low heat until milk steams. Do not boil.

Melissa Fraser, Valencia, CA

Cinnamon Crisps

These crisps are a great little treat for a mid-afternoon snack.

Serves 8

1/2 t. vanilla extract
1 T. hot water
1/2 t. cinnamon
3 T. sugar
4 6-inch flour tortillas, each cut into 8 wedges

Combine vanilla and water in a cup; blend cinnamon and sugar in a separate cup. Brush vanilla mixture over both sides of tortilla wedges; sprinkle with cinnamon-sugar. Place on a baking sheet sprayed with non-stick vegetable spray. Bake at 450 degrees for 5 minutes, until crisp.

Lisa Ashton, Aston, PA

Chocolate Pinwheels

We love to serve these yummy treats with Warm Spiced Milk...the perfect combination!

Makes 16

11-oz. tube refrigerated bread sticks
3/4 c. semi-sweet chocolate chips
1/4 c. butter, melted
1/2 c. sugar

Unroll bread sticks and cut them in half. Press chocolate chips in a single row along the top of each bread stick half; roll up into a pinwheel shape. Arrange pinwheels on a parchment paperlined baking sheet. Brush with melted butter; sprinkle with sugar. Bake at 350 degrees for 10 to 12 minutes, until golden.

Flavor Options
Try other fillings for your pinwheels such as dried cranberries, raisins and nuts. If you prefer savory snacks, try shredded cheese or bits of crispy fried bacon.

Chocolate Pinwheels with Warm Spiced Milk

Cindy Elliott, Modesto, IL

Honey-Glazed Snack Mix

Pack in plastic bags for school-day snacks, then keep some for yourself to go with mid-morning coffee.

Makes about 10 cups

5 c. crispy corn & rice cereal squares
3 c. mini pretzel twists
2 c. pecan halves
1/2 c. honey
1/2 c. butter, melted

Combine cereal, pretzels and pecans in a large bowl; set aside. Blend together honey and butter. Pour over cereal mixture; toss to coat. Spread on ungreased baking sheets. Bake at 300 degrees for 10 minutes. Stir and continue to bake an additional 10 to 15 minutes. Pour onto wax paper, and cool completely. Store in airtight containers.

Georgia Muth, Penn Valley, CA

Cranberry-Pecan Coffee Cakes

These tender cranberry-and-nut streusel loaves are perfect to serve with coffee or tea.

Makes 4 mini coffee cakes

1/2 c. butter, softened
1 c. sugar
2 eggs
2 c. all-purpose flour
2 t. baking powder
1/2 t. baking soda
1/2 t. salt
8-oz. container sour cream
1 t. almond extract
1 t. vanilla extract
16-oz. can whole-berry cranberry
  sauce
1 c. coarsely chopped pecans

Beat butter at medium speed with an electric mixer until creamy. Gradually add sugar, beating well. Add eggs, one at a time, beating until blended after each addition. Combine flour, baking powder, baking soda and salt. Add flour mixture to butter mixture alternately with sour cream, beginning and ending with flour mixture. Stir in extracts. Spoon 1/2 cup batter into each of 4 greased and floured 5"x3" mini loaf pans. Gently stir cranberry sauce; spoon 3 tablespoons over batter in each pan and spread lightly to edges; sprinkle 2 tablespoons pecans over cranberry sauce in each pan. Repeat layers in each pan using remaining batter, cranberry sauce and pecans. Bake at 350 degrees for 48 to 50 minutes, until a toothpick inserted in center comes out clean. Cool in pans on a wire rack 15 minutes; remove from pans and let cool completely. Drizzle Almond Cream Glaze over cooled cakes.

ALMOND CREAM GLAZE

3/4 c. powdered sugar
2 T. whipping cream
1/2 t. almond extract

Stir together all ingredients.

Cranberry-Pecan Coffee Cakes

Sharon Velenosi, Costa Mesa, CA

Whole-Wheat Soda Bread

A wonderful hearty, coarse-textured bread that pairs well with a cup of hot tea. Add just a little honey on top for a sweet treat.

Serves 4

1 c. all-purpose flour
1 t. baking powder
1 t. baking soda
1/2 t. salt
2 T. sugar
2 c. whole-wheat flour
1-1/2 c. buttermilk
1 T. butter, melted

In a large bowl, combine all-purpose flour, baking powder, baking soda, salt and sugar. Add whole-wheat flour; mix well. Add buttermilk; stir just until moistened. Turn dough onto a floured surface. Knead gently for about 2 minutes, until well mixed and dough is smooth. Form dough into a ball; pat into a circle and place in a lightly greased cast-iron skillet. With a floured knife, mark dough into 4 wedges by cutting halfway through to the bottom. Transfer skillet to oven. Bake, uncovered, at 375 degrees for 30 to 40 minutes, until loaf sounds hollow when tapped. Brush with butter; cool on a wire rack.

Judy Renkievich, Grand Marais, MN

Rosemary-Lemon Scones

Fresh rosemary and lemon zest are the secret ingredients in these flaky scones.

Makes 8 scones

2 c. all-purpose flour
2 T. sugar
1 T. baking powder
2 t. fresh rosemary, chopped
2 t. lemon zest
1/4 t. salt
1/4 c. butter
2 eggs, beaten
1/2 c. whipping cream
Garnish: additional whipping
    cream, additional sugar

Combine flour, sugar, baking power, rosemary, lemon zest and salt in a large mixing bowl. With a pastry blender or 2 knives, cut in butter until mixture is crumbly. Combine eggs and whipping cream in a medium bowl; add to flour mixture and stir well. (Dough may be sticky.) Knead dough lightly 4 times on a well-floured surface. Shape dough into an 8-inch circle about 1/2-inch thick. Place dough on a lightly greased baking sheet. Cut circle into wedges; do not separate wedges. Brush additional cream over top of scones and sprinkle with additional sugar. Bake at 425 degrees for 14 minutes or until golden.

Rosemary-Lemon Scones

Jackie Smulski, Lyons, IL

Orange & Walnut Brunch Cake

Don't save this delectable cake just for special occasions...enjoy it anytime!

Serves 6 to 8

16.3-oz. tube refrigerated
  jumbo biscuits
1/4 c. walnuts, finely chopped
1/3 c. sugar
1 T. orange zest
2 T. butter, melted
1/2 c. powdered sugar
3 T. cream cheese, softened
2 T. orange juice

Grease a 9" round cake pan. Separate biscuit dough into 8 biscuits. Place one biscuit in center of pan. Cut remaining biscuits in half, forming 14 half-circles. Arrange pieces around center biscuit, with cut sides facing same direction. Combine walnuts, sugar and orange zest in a small bowl; mix well. Brush butter over tops of biscuits and sprinkle with walnut mixture. Bake at 375 degrees for 20 minutes, until golden. In a separate bowl, combine powdered sugar, cream cheese and enough orange juice for desired drizzling consistency. Blend until smooth; drizzle over warm cake. Cool for 10 minutes. Serve warm.

Corinne Gross, Tigard, OR

Ginger-Carrot Bread

The zucchini in this bread keeps it moist and yummy!

Serves 16

3 c. all-purpose flour
2 t. cinnamon
1-1/2 t. ground ginger
1/4 t. baking powder
1 t. baking soda
2/3 c. crystallized ginger, finely
  diced
3 eggs
1 c. canola oil
1-3/4 c. sugar
2 t. vanilla extract
1 c. carrots, peeled and grated
1 c. zucchini, yellow or pattypan
  squash, grated

In a bowl, sift together flour, spices, baking powder and baking soda. Stir in crystallized ginger; set aside. In a separate large bowl, with an electric mixer on medium speed, beat eggs until light and foamy, about 2 minutes. Add oil, sugar and vanilla; beat until sugar dissolves. Add carrots and squash; mix gently until combined. Add flour mixture to egg mixture; stir gently. Coat two, 8-1/2"x4-1/2" loaf pans with non-stick vegetable spray. Spoon batter into pans. Bake at 325 degrees for about one hour, until firm and a toothpick tests clean. Cool loaves in pans on a wire rack for 15 minutes. Remove from pans; cool completely on rack.

Ginger-Carrot Bread

Vickie, Gooseberry Patch

Mocha Coffee

This rich and creamy coffee is super easy to make and it is always a hit. Who doesn't love the flavor combination of coffee, cream and chocolate? Yum!

Makes 10 servings

6 T. plus 2 t. instant espresso coffee
   powder
1-1/4 c. powdered non-dairy creamer
1/2 c. plus 2 t. sugar
3 T. plus 1 t. baking cocoa
1 T. vanilla powder

Combine all ingredients, stirring well. Store in an airtight container. For each serving, add 3/4 cup boiling water to 1/4 cup mix; stir well.

Kelly Marshall, Olathe, KS

Kelly's Easy Caramel Rolls

This is a much-requested family recipe! It is the perfect treat to serve with a hot cup of coffee after working outside all morning.

Makes 10 rolls

3 T. corn syrup, divided
3 T. brown sugar, packed and divided
3 T. chopped pecans, divided
2 T. butter, cubed and divided
12-oz. tube refrigerated biscuits

To each of 10 greased muffin cups, add one teaspoon each of syrup, brown sugar and pecans. Top each with 1/2 teaspoon butter and one biscuit. Bake at 400 degrees for 8 to 10 minutes, until golden. Invert rolls onto a plate before serving.

Mocha Coffee

Kelly's Easy Caramel Rolls

Donna Wilson, Maryville, TN

Glazed Pumpkin Scones

I absolutely love pumpkin and scones! These smell so yummy when baking, and taste even better when done. One of my sneaky ways to get kids to eat vegetables.

Makes 8 scones

2 c. all-purpose flour
1/2 c. sugar
1 T. baking powder
1/2 t. salt
1-1/2 t. pumpkin pie spice
1/2 c. butter, diced
1/2 c. canned pumpkin
3 T. milk
1 egg, beaten

Combine flour, sugar, baking powder, salt and spice in a large bowl. Cut in butter with a pastry blender until crumbly; set aside. In a separate bowl, whisk together pumpkin, milk and egg. Fold pumpkin mixture into flour mixture. Form dough into a ball; pat out dough onto a floured surface. Form into a 9-inch circle. Cut into 8 wedges and place on a greased baking sheet. Bake at 425 degrees for 14 to 16 minutes. Drizzle scones with Powdered Sugar Glaze; allow to set.

POWDERED SUGAR GLAZE
1 c. powdered sugar
2 to 3 T. milk
1/2 t. pumpkin pie spice

Mix all ingredients together, adding enough milk for a drizzling consistency.

Leslie Williams, Americus, GA

Maple-Pecan Brunch Ring

A sweet & simple way to make a tasty treat for guests.

Makes about 12 servings

3/4 c. chopped pecans
1/2 c. brown sugar, packed
2 t. cinnamon
2 17.3-oz. tubes refrigerated jumbo flaky biscuits
2 T. butter, melted
1/2 c. maple syrup

Combine pecans, brown sugar and cinnamon; set aside. Split each biscuit horizontally; brush half of the biscuits with butter and sprinkle with half the pecan mixture. Arrange topped biscuits in a circle on an ungreased baking sheet; overlap each biscuit slightly and keep within 2 inches of the edge of the baking sheet. Brush remaining biscuit halves with butter; sprinkle with remaining pecan mixture. Arrange a second ring just inside the first ring, overlapping edges. Bake at 350 degrees for 30 to 35 minutes, until golden. Remove to wire rack; cool 10 minutes. Brush with maple syrup.

Maple-Pecan Brunch Ring

Mary Ary, Lexington, KY

English Cider

This warm and spicy drink is yummy any time of year, but especially when winter is in the air!

Makes 6 to 8 servings

1/2 c. brown sugar, packed
1-1/2 qts. apple cider
1 t. whole allspice
2 cinnamon sticks
2 t. whole cloves
1 orange, sliced and seeded

Combine ingredients in a large stockpot. Spices can be placed in a tea strainer, if preferred, or added loose. Cover and simmer for 25 minutes. Strain before serving if necessary.

English Cider

Sandy Bernards, Valencia, CA

Miss Karen's Coffee Cake

The Greek yogurt in this recipe makes it so moist and rich. This coffee cake is always a must when serving coffee to family & friends.

Serves 15

2-1/4 c. all-purpose flour
3/4 c. brown sugar, packed
3/4 c. butter, diced
8-oz. container plain low-fat
   Greek yogurt
1 egg, beaten
1 t. vanilla extract
1/4 t. ground ginger
1 t. baking soda
3 T. sugar
1 t. cinnamon
1 c. chopped pecans

Mix together flour and brown sugar in a large bowl; cut in butter until crumbly. Press 2-3/4 cups of mixture into a greased 13"x9" baking pan; set aside remaining mixture. In a separate bowl, combine yogurt, egg, vanilla, ginger and baking soda; add remaining crumbly mixture. Pour over crust. In a small bowl, combine sugar, cinnamon and pecans; sprinkle over yogurt mixture. Bake at 350 degrees for 25 to 30 minutes.

Miss Karen's Coffee Cake

Brenda Hughes, Houston, TX

Gorilla Bread

Like monkey bread, but better... everyone will ask for second helpings and even thirds when you serve this recipe!

Serves 20

1/2 c. sugar
1 T. cinnamon
1 c. butter
2 c. brown sugar, packed
2 12-oz. tubes refrigerated biscuits
8-oz. pkg. cream cheese, cut into
    20 cubes
1-1/2 c. walnuts, coarsely chopped
    and divided

Mix sugar and cinnamon; set aside. Melt butter and brown sugar in a saucepan over low heat, stirring well; set aside. Flatten biscuits; sprinkle each with 1/2 teaspoon sugar mixture. Place a cheese cube in the center of each biscuit, wrapping and sealing dough around cheese. Set aside. Spray a 12-cup Bundt® pan with non-stick vegetable spray; sprinkle 1/2 cup nuts in the bottom of pan. Arrange half the biscuits in the pan. Sprinkle with half the sugar mixture; pour half the butter mixture over top and sprinkle with 1/2 cup nuts. Repeat layers with remaining biscuits, sugar mixture, butter mixture and nuts. Bake at 350 degrees for 30 minutes. Let cool 5 minutes; place a plate on top and invert.

Bonnie Allard, Santa Rosa, CA

Peach Cobbler Cupcakes

My most-requested muffin-like cupcakes...my family & friends love them! They disappear right away whenever I make them to share. We like them with a cup of hot tea.

Makes 1-1/2 dozen

3 c. all-purpose flour
1 c. sugar
1-1/2 T. baking soda
1/2 t. salt
3/4 c. butter, diced
1-3/4 c. milk
15-oz. can sliced peaches, drained
    and chopped
Optional: brown sugar

Mix flour, sugar, baking soda and salt in a large bowl. Cut in butter with a pastry blender or a fork. Add milk and peaches; stir just until moistened. Spoon batter into 18 greased muffin cups, filling 2/3 full. Add one teaspoon of brown sugar into the center of each cupcake if desired. Bake at 400 degrees for 15 to 20 minutes, until golden. Turn out and cool slightly on a wire rack; serve warm or cooled.

Peach Cobbler Cupcakes

Nola Coons, Gooseberry Patch

Cranberry Tea

A special treat for tea lovers. So yummy with your favorite scones!

Makes 4 quarts

6 c. water, divided
2 family-size or 8 regular teabags
1 t. whole cloves
2 2-1/2 inch cinnamon sticks
2 c. sugar
2 c. cranberry juice cocktail
1 c. orange juice
1/4 c. lemon juice

In a large pot, bring 4 cups water to a boil. Add teabags, cloves and cinnamon sticks; cover and steep for 5 minutes. Strain, discarding teabags and spices. Stir in remaining water and other ingredients. Stir until sugar is dissolved. Serve warm or over ice.

Barb Schoenholtz, Reeds Spring, MO

Sweet Fruit & Almond Scones

When I bake these scones, they bring back memories of good times and my kids enjoying them with fresh butter and jam. Delicious!

Makes 10 scones

2 c. all-purpose flour
1/4 c. sugar, divided
1 T. baking powder
1/4 t. salt
6 T. chilled butter, diced
2 eggs, lightly beaten
1/2 c. plus 1 T. 2% milk, divided
1/2 c. dried cranberries and
    blueberries
1/2 c. sliced toasted almonds

In a large bowl, sift together flour, 3 tablespoons sugar, baking powder and salt; set aside. Use a fork or pastry blender to cut in butter until very small pieces form. Make a well in the center; set aside. In a separate bowl, whisk eggs and 1/2 cup milk together. Pour egg mixture into well in flour mixture. Stir lightly with a fork until dough comes together. Add berries and nuts; mix together. Turn out dough onto a lightly floured surface. With floured hands, gently pat dough into an 8-inch circle, about 3/8-inch thick. Cut circle into 10 wedges; transfer to a parchment paper-lined baking sheet. Brush tops with remaining milk and sprinkle with remaining sugar. Bake at 400 degrees for 15 to 20 minutes, until golden. Cool on a wire rack. Drizzle with Powdered Sugar Frosting.

POWDERED SUGAR FROSTING
1 c. powdered sugar
1 T. milk

Mix together to the consistency of heavy cream.

Sweet Fruit & Almond Scones

Kendall Hale, Lynn, MA

Pumpkin Spice Bars

Watch these bars disappear fast!

Makes 2 dozen

18-1/4 oz. pkg. spice cake mix
1/2 c. plus 1 T. butter, melted and
　divided
1/2 c. pecans, finely chopped
1 T. plus 1 t. vanilla extract, divided
8-oz. pkg. cream cheese, softened
1/3 c. light brown sugar, packed
1 c. canned pumpkin
1 egg, beaten
1/2 c. white chocolate, finely
　chopped
1/3 c. long-cooking oats, uncooked
Optional: powdered sugar

Combine cake mix, 1/2 cup melted butter, pecans and one tablespoon vanilla, mixing with a fork. Reserve one cup crumbs for streusel topping. Press remaining crumbs into a lightly greased 13"x9" baking pan. Bake at 350 degrees for about 13 to 15 minutes, until puffy and set. Cool in pan on a wire rack 20 minutes. Beat cream cheese at medium speed with an electric mixer 30 seconds or until creamy. Add brown sugar, pumpkin, egg and remaining vanilla; beat until blended. Pour filling over baked crust. Stir white chocolate, remaining melted butter and oats into reserved streusel. Sprinkle over filling. Bake at 350 degrees for 30 minutes or until edges begin to brown and center is set. Cool completely in pan on a wire rack. Sprinkle with powdered sugar, if desired. Cut into bars. Serve at room temperature or chilled.

Brenda Smith, Delaware, OH

Taffy Apple Pizza

An after-school treat I used to make for my kids when they were little. We'd enjoy this tasty dessert together while catching up on their day. Now I make it for special parties and when friends drop in.

Makes 8 to 10 servings

18-oz. pkg. refrigerated sugar cookie
　dough
8-oz. pkg. cream cheese, softened
1/2 c. brown sugar, packed
1/4 c. creamy or crunchy peanut
　butter
1 t. vanilla extract
2 Granny Smith apples, peeled,
　cored and sliced
1/4 c. caramel ice cream topping
1/2 c. chopped peanuts

Form cookie dough into a ball; place in the center of a greased 14" round pizza pan. Using a lightly floured rolling pin, roll out to a 14-inch circle, about 1/4-inch thick. Bake at 350 degrees for 16 to 18 minutes, until lightly golden. Remove from oven; cool 10 minutes. Slightly loosen cookie from pan with a serrated knife; set aside. In a bowl, combine cream cheese, brown sugar, peanut butter and vanilla; mix well and spread evenly over cookie. Arrange apple slices evenly over cream cheese mixture. Microwave topping on high setting for 30 to 45 seconds, until warm; drizzle evenly over apples. Sprinkle with peanuts; cut into wedges to serve.

Taffy Apple Pizza

Linda Behling, Cecil, PA

Chai Tea

The spices in this tea make it a cozy companion to any sweet goodie.

Serves 20

1 c. non-fat dry milk powder
1 c. powdered non-dairy creamer
1/2 c. sugar
2 t. ground ginger
1 t. ground cloves
1 t. ground cardamom
brewed black tea

In a large bowl, combine all ingredients except tea. To serve, add 2 tablespoons of mixture to one cup of brewed tea.

Beth Kramer, Port Saint Lucie, FL

Orange Coffee Rolls

Serve these rolls with a cup of coffee for a special mid-morning treat.

Makes 2 dozen

1 env. active dry yeast
1/4 c. warm water
1 c. sugar, divided
2 eggs, beaten
1/2 c. sour cream
1/2 c. butter, melted and divided
1 t. salt
2-3/4 to 3 c. all-purpose flour
1 c. flaked coconut, toasted and
     divided
2 T. orange zest

Combine yeast and warm water (110 to 115 degrees) in a large bowl; let stand 5 minutes. Add 1/4 cup sugar, eggs, sour cream, 6 tablespoons melted butter and salt; beat at medium speed with an electric mixer until blended. Gradually stir in enough flour to make a soft dough. Turn dough out onto a well-floured surface; knead until smooth and elastic (about 5 minutes). Place in a well greased bowl, turning to grease top. Cover and let rise in a warm place (85 degrees), free from drafts, 1-1/2 hours or until doubled in bulk. Punch dough down and divide in half. Roll one portion of dough into a 12-inch circle; brush with one tablespoon melted butter. Combine remaining sugar, 3/4 cup coconut and orange zest; sprinkle half of coconut mixture over dough. Cut into 12 wedges; roll up each wedge, beginning at wide end. Place in a greased 13"x9" baking pan, point side down. Repeat with remaining dough, butter and coconut mixture. Cover and let rise in a warm place, free from drafts, 45 minutes or until doubled in bulk. Bake at 350 degrees for 25 to 30 minutes, until golden. (Cover with aluminum foil after 15 minutes to prevent excessive browning, if necessary.) Spoon warm Glaze over warm rolls; sprinkle with remaining coconut.

GLAZE

3/4 c. sugar
1/2 c. sour cream
1/4 c. butter
2 t. orange juice

Combine all ingredients in a small saucepan; bring to a boil. Boil 3 minutes, stirring occasionally. Let Cool slightly.

Orange Coffee Rolls

Creamy Chicken & Biscuits

CHAPTER FOUR

Come to Dinner

You've had a busy day and now it's time to
gather at the table for dinner and enjoy
some tasty dishes and family time together.

Mongolian Beef, Page 176

Dijon Chicken & Fresh Herbs, Page 172

Marcia Wolff, Rolling Prairie, IN

Delicious Dill Bread

This bread is easy to make and has such a fresh flavor and delicate texture. Serve it with your favorite main dish.

Serves 14

1/3 c. warm water
1 env. active dry yeast
1 c. cottage cheese
1 T. butter, softened
1 T. fresh chives, chopped
2 t. dill weed
2 t. salt
1 T. sugar
1/4 t. baking soda
1 egg, beaten
2 to 2-1/2 c. all-purpose or bread
    flour
Garnish: additional butter

Heat water until very warm, about 110 to 115 degrees. Add yeast to water and let stand for 5 minutes. Place cottage cheese in a large microwave-safe dish; heat until warmed.

Add butter, chives, dill weed and salt to cottage cheese. Add yeast mixture and stir; add sugar, baking soda, egg and enough flour to make a stiff dough. Cover and let rise in a warm place until doubled. Punch down; dough will be sticky. Transfer into two well-greased round casserole dishes or two, 9"x5" loaf pans. Bake at 350 degrees for 45 to 50 minutes. If bread is browning too quickly, cover lightly with aluminum foil. Remove from oven; rub butter over top if desired.

Cris Goode, Mooresville, IN

Good & Healthy "Fried" Chicken

We love this healthier version of everyone's favorite food...fried chicken!

Makes 5 servings

1 c. whole-grain panko bread crumbs
1 c. cornmeal
2 T. all-purpose flour
salt and pepper to taste
1 c. buttermilk
10 chicken drumsticks

Combine panko, cornmeal, flour, salt and pepper in a gallon-size plastic zipping bag. Coat chicken with buttermilk, one piece at a time. Drop chicken into bag and shake to coat pieces lightly. Arrange chicken in one to two 13"x9" baking pans coated with non-stick vegetable spray. Bake, uncovered, at 350 degrees for 40 to 50 minutes, until chicken juices run clear.

Delicious Dill Bread

Good & Healthy "Fried" Chicken

Ginny Paccioretti, Oak Ridge, NJ

Eggplant Ratatouille

This southern French dish is made with eggplant, zucchini, onions, peppers, tomato and garlic. There are many different variations, but this recipe is my favorite!

Makes 8 servings

1 onion, chopped
3 cloves garlic, chopped
3 T. olive oil
2 zucchini, sliced
2 eggplants, peeled and cubed
1 green peppers, sliced
28-oz. can crushed tomatoes
1 t. dried parsley
1 t. dried oregano
1 t. dried basil
3 c. hot cooked brown rice

Sauté onion and garlic in oil in large skillet over medium heat. Add remaining ingredients, except rice; simmer over medium heat for 30 minutes or until vegetables are tender. Serve over cooked rice.

Recipe and Photo Courtesy of BeefItsWhatsForDinner.com

Beef & Asparagus Toss

So light and delicious, this will be your go-to dinner.

Serves 4

1 lb. lean ground beef
3 c. bow tie pasta, uncooked
1 lb. fresh asparagus, cut into 1-inch pieces
1 T. olive oil
1/4 c. shallots, minced
1 T. garlic, minced
salt and pepper to taste
Garnish: 1/4 c. shredded Parmesan cheese

Cook pasta in salted boiling water 10 minutes or until almost tender. Add asparagus; continue cooking 3 to 4 minutes or until pasta and asparagus are tender. Drain well. Meanwhile, heat large nonstick skillet over medium heat until hot. Add beef; cook 8 to 10 minutes, breaking into 3/4-inch crumbles and stirring occasionally. Remove from skillet with slotted spoon; pour off drippings. Heat oil in same skillet over medium heat until hot. Add shallots and garlic; cook 3 to 4 minutes or until tender, stirring frequently. Remove from heat. Add beef; toss to mix. Season with salt and pepper, as desired. Combine beef mixture with pasta and asparagus in large bowl; toss well. Sprinkle with cheese.

Beef & Asparagus Toss

Angie Dixon, Pevely, MO

Beef & Noodle Skillet

This is a hearty and zesty dish to warm your tummy.

Serves 4

1 lb. ground beef
2 10-1/2 oz. cans beef broth
8-oz. pkg. elbow macaroni
16-oz. pkg. pasteurized process cheese spread, cubed
1 c. salsa

Brown beef in a large skillet over medium heat; drain. Add broth; heat to boiling; stir in macaroni. Boil until macaroni is tender; reduce heat and mix in cheese and salsa. Heat through, stirring occasionally until cheese melts.

Deborah Clouser, McLean, VA

Creamy Chicken & Biscuits

You can see the smiles on the faces of my entire family when I take this dish out of the oven. It doesn't take long to make and it is so good!

Serves 8

2 c. new redskin potatoes, halved or quartered
2 c. carrots, peeled and sliced
1 onion, diced
3 T. butter
3 T. all-purpose flour
salt and pepper to taste
2 c. milk
1 c. chicken broth
2 cubes chicken bouillon
2 boneless, skinless chicken breasts, cooked and diced
12-oz. tube large refrigerated biscuits, cut into quarters

Cover potatoes, carrots and onion with water in a medium saucepan. Bring to a boil over medium heat; reduce heat and simmer until tender. Drain and set aside. Melt butter in another medium saucepan; stir in flour, salt and pepper, stirring constantly. Gradually add milk, broth and bouillon. Cook until thickened, about 3 to 5 minutes; set aside. Combine chicken and vegetables in a lightly greased 13"x9" baking pan. Pour sauce over top; arrange biscuits over sauce. Bake, uncovered, at 400 degrees for 15 minutes, or until biscuits are golden and sauce is bubbly.

Creamy Chicken & Biscuits

Ursula Juarez-Wall, Dumfries, VA

Delicious Quick Rolls

My Grandma Bohannon is the most amazing woman I know! Not a single holiday meal passed without Grandma's piping-hot rolls.

Makes one dozen

1 c. water
1 env. active dry yeast
2 T. sugar
2 T. shortening, melted
1 egg, beaten
2-1/4 c. all-purpose flour
1 t. salt

Heat water until very warm, about 110 to 115 degrees. In a large bowl, dissolve yeast in warm water. Add remaining ingredients; beat until smooth. Cover and let rise until double in size, about 30 to 60 minutes. Punch down. Form dough into 12 balls and place in a greased muffin pan. Cover and let rise again until double, about 30 minutes. Bake at 350 degrees for 15 minutes, or until golden.

Delicious Quick Rolls

Lisanne Miller, Wells, ME

3-Cheese Pasta Bake

This yummy mac & cheese dish gets a great update with penne pasta and a trio of cheeses.

Serves 4

8-oz. pkg. penne pasta, uncooked
2 T. butter
2 T. all-purpose flour
1-1/2 c. milk
1/2 c. half-and-half
1 c. shredded white Cheddar cheese
1/4 c. grated Parmesan cheese
2 c. shredded Gruyère cheese,
    divided
1 t. salt
1/4 t. pepper
1/8 t. nutmeg

Prepare pasta according to package directions; drain. Meanwhile, melt butter in a saucepan over medium heat. Whisk in flour until smooth; cook, whisking constantly, one minute. Gradually whisk in milk and half-and-half; cook, whisking constantly, 3 to 5 minutes or until thickened. Stir in Cheddar cheese, Parmesan cheese, one cup Gruyère cheese and next 3 ingredients and seasonings until smooth. Stir together pasta and cheese mixture; pour into a lightly greased 11"x7" baking pan. Top with remaining Gruyère cheese. Bake, uncovered, at 350 degrees for about 15 minutes or until golden and bubbly.

3-Cheese Pasta Bake

Shannon Hildebrandt, Ontario, Canada

Ground Beef & Kale Curry

While on holiday, my husband and I stayed with our friends Pete and Liz, who are Kenyan nationals. They wanted us to experience Kenyan cuisine and introduced us to a version of this delicious dish. Madras curry powder is spicy, so add a little or a lot as you prefer.

Serves 4

1 lb. ground beef
1/2 c. onion, chopped
3 cloves garlic, minced
28-oz. can diced tomatoes
1 bunch fresh kale, torn and stalks
    removed
1/2 to 1 T. hot Madras curry powder
salt and pepper to taste
Optional: cooked basmati rice or
    couscous

In a large skillet over medium heat, cook beef, onion and garlic until beef is no longer pink. Stir in tomatoes with juice and kale; add desired amount of curry powder. Reduce heat to low. Cover and simmer for about 15 minutes, stirring occasionally. Season with salt and pepper. Serve plain or over cooked basmati rice or couscous.

Carol Field Dahlstrom, Ankeny, IA

BLT Kabobs

These kabobs make a light dinner that is tasty and fun to eat.

Serves 4

1 lb. thick-sliced bacon
metal skewers
2 small red tomatoes, quartered
2 small yellow tomatoes, quartered
1 avocado, peeled and pitted
4 slices bread, toasted
bamboo skewers
pepper to taste
Garnish: lettuce leaves

Preheat oven to 375 degrees. Prepare the bacon by accordian-folding the bacon onto metal skewers. Place on baking sheet on rack and cook until bacon is brown and fully cooked. Leave on skewers to cool slightly. Place avocado in a bowl and mash slightly. Spread 2 pieces of bread with avocado. Top with other pieces of bread, making 2 sandwiches. Cut sandwiches into 4 pieces each; set aside. Soak the bamboo skewers in water for about 5 minutes. Remove bacon from skewers; carefully thread several pieces onto bamboo skewers. Add the sandwich pieces, tomatoes, more bacon, tomato and sandwich pieces in desired order and amount. Place on a baking sheet; sprinkle with pepper if desired. Heat broiler to low. Place skewers under broiler until just heated, about one minute, watching carefully so kabobs do not burn. Serve immediately on lettuce leaves.

BLT Kabobs

Recipe and Photo Courtesy
National Pork Board

Herbed Pork Ribeye Roast with Cauliflower

Ask the butcher to trim away the meat from the ends of the bones for a delicious presentation. To make the preparation even easier, look for pre-cut cauliflower flowerets.

Serves 8

4 t. dried thyme or 1/4 c. fresh
    thyme, chopped
1-1/2 t. salt
1-1/2 t. pepper
8-rib pork ribeye roast (rack of
    pork)
8 c. cauliflower flowerets
4 shallots, sliced
3 slices bacon, cut crosswise into
    1/4-inch slices

Preheat the oven to 375 degrees. Arrange one oven rack in the lower third of the oven and one in the upper third. In a small bowl, combine thyme, salt and pepper. Set 2 teaspoons of herb mixture aside (or 5 teaspoons if using fresh thyme); sprinkle remaining mixture over all sides of the pork. Place pork fat-side up in a shallow roasting pan, and then place pan on lower oven rack. Bake for one to 2 hours, until a meat thermometer inserted in thickest part reaches between 145 degrees (medium rare) to 160 degrees (medium), one to 2 hours. About 30 minutes before pork is done, in a large bowl, combine cauliflower, shallots and reserved herb mixture. Transfer to a rimmed baking sheet and scatter bacon on top. Place baking sheet on upper oven rack. Bake for 40 minutes, until cauliflower is tender and bacon is browned. Meanwhile, make Chardonnay Butter Sauce. Remove roast from oven and let rest 10 minutes. (Cauliflower will continue cooking; it should be done when the roast is finished resting). Slice roast between the rib bones. Serve drizzled with pan juices, and with cauliflower and sauce on the side.

CHARDONNAY BUTTER SAUCE
1 c. Chardonnay or other dry white
    wine or apple juice
1/3 c. whipping cream
2 shallots, finely diced
6 T. cold butter, cut into 10 pieces
salt and pepper to taste

In a medium saucepan over medium-high heat, combine wine or apple juice, cream and shallots; bring to a boil. Cook; stirring occasionally, until reduced to 2/3 cup, about 10 minutes (adjust heat to avoid boiling over). Remove from heat and whisk in butter, 2 or 3 pieces at a time, waiting until the pieces are melted before adding more. Add salt and pepper to taste. Cover to keep warm; set aside.

Herbed Pork Ribeye Roast with Cauliflower

Tina George, Eldorado, AR

Santa Fe Chicken & Potatoes

This five-ingredient recipe is simple to prepare on busy nights when you're pressed for time! It smells so good when it's cooking, and it's easy to double for my large family.

Serves 4

**4 potatoes, peeled and cut into
   3/4-inch cubes
1 lb. boneless, skinless chicken
   breasts, cut into 3/4-inch cubes
2 T. olive oil
1 c. salsa
11-oz. can corn, drained**

Place potatoes in a microwave-safe dish; add a small amount of water. Cover with plastic wrap; vent and microwave on high for 8 to 10 minutes, until tender. Meanwhile, in a large skillet over high heat, sauté chicken in oil over medium-high heat for 5 minutes. Add potatoes; sauté and toss until potatoes are lightly golden. Stir in salsa and corn; toss until heated through.

Donna Deeds, Marysville, TN

Chicken-Fried Steak

Authentic chicken-fried steak is crunchy outside, tender inside and served with plenty of creamy gravy!

Serves 6

**2-1/4 t. salt, divided
1-3/4 t. pepper, divided
6 4-oz. beef cube steaks
1 sleeve saltine crackers, crushed
1-1/4 c. all-purpose flour, divided
1/2 t. baking powder
1/2 t. cayenne pepper
4-3/4 c. milk, divided
2 eggs, beaten
3-1/2 c. peanut oil
mashed potatoes**

Sprinkle 1/4 teaspoon each salt and pepper over steaks. Set aside. Combine cracker crumbs, one cup flour, baking powder, one teaspoon salt, 1/2 teaspoon pepper and cayenne pepper. Whisk together 3/4 cup milk and eggs. Dredge steaks in cracker crumb mixture; dip in milk mixture and dredge in cracker mixture again. Pour oil into a 12" skillet and heat to 360 degrees. Fry steaks, in batches, 10 minutes. Turn and fry each batch 4 to 5 more minutes or until golden. Remove to a wire rack on a jelly-roll pan. Keep steaks warm in a 225-degree oven. Carefully drain hot oil, reserving cooked bits and one tablespoon drippings in skillet. Whisk together remaining flour, salt, pepper and milk. Pour mixture into reserved drippings in skillet; cook over medium-high heat, whisking constantly, 10 to 12 minutes or until thickened. Serve gravy with steaks and mashed potatoes.

Chicken-Fried Steak

Devi McDonald, Visalia, CA

Skillet Apples & Pork Chops

Juicy pan-seared pork chops are paired with sautéed apples and onion...very satisfying.

Makes 6 servings

6 bone-in pork chops
salt and pepper to taste
1/4 c. butter, divided
3 to 4 Granny Smith apples, cored
    and thinly sliced
1 onion, thinly sliced
1/2 t. fresh thyme, chopped
1 c. lager-style beer or apple cider

Season pork chops with salt and pepper. Melt half of butter in a skillet over medium-high heat. Add pork chops to skillet; cook for 5 minutes. Turn chops over and cook for another 4 minutes, or until juices run clear. Drain; remove chops to a plate. Reduce heat to medium; add remaining butter, apples, onion and thyme to skillet. Cook for about 6 minutes, stirring occasionally; add beer or cider. Cook an additional 15 minutes, or until liquid has reduced and thickened. Return chops to skillet; cover with apple mixture. Cook for 5 minutes. Serve chops topped with apple mixture.

Recipe and Photo Courtesy
National Pork Board

Midwestern Pork Tenderloin Sandwich

The "tender" in the name of this sandwich refers to the ease with which you can sink your teeth into it. The cut of pork is actually boneless loin, "tenderized" with a meat mallet.

Serves 4

1 lb. boneless pork loin or boneless
    pork chops
1 c. all-purpose flour
1/2 c. yellow cornmeal
1 t. salt
1/2 t. pepper
oil for frying
4 large sandwich buns, split
Garnish: mustard, mayonnaise,
    pickle, catsup, sliced onion,
    lettuce leaves

Cut 4 one-inch slices of pork. Trim fat from edges; butterfly each slice by cutting horizontally through the middle almost to the edge, so that the halves are connected by only a thick piece of meat. Put each butterflied slice between pieces of plastic wrap. Using a wooden meat mallet, or the side of a cleaver, pound vigorously until the slice is about 10 inches across. Mix together flour, cornmeal, salt and pepper. Heat 1/2 inch of oil in a deep, wide skillet to 365 degrees. Dip each slice of pork in water, then in flour mixture. Fry tenderloin, turning once, until golden brown on both sides, about 5 minutes total. Drain on paper towels. Serve on buns, garnished as desired.

Midwestern Pork Tenderloin Sandwich

Kendall Hall, Lynn, MA

Whole Acorn Squash Cream Soup

This unique recipe celebrates the beauty of squash by using it as a serving bowl. Choose squash that stand upright for ease in baking and serving.

Serves 4

4 acorn squash
1/4 c. cream cheese
1 c. whipping cream
1 c. chicken broth
1/2 t. salt
1 t. cinnamon

Cut off about one inch of stem ends of squash to reveal seeds. Scoop out and discard seeds and pulp. Arrange squash in an ungreased 13"x9" baking pan. Place one tablespoon cream cheese in each squash. Pour 1/4 cup each whipping cream and chicken broth over cream cheese in each squash; sprinkle each with 1/8 teaspoon salt and 1/4 teaspoon cinnamon. Add 1/2 inch of water to baking pan. Bake, uncovered, at 350 degrees for one hour and 45 minutes, or until squash are very tender. To serve, carefully set each squash in a shallow soup bowl.

Stacie Avner, Delaware, OH

Dijon Chicken & Fresh Herbs

I love making this family favorite in the summertime with my fresh garden herbs.

Serves 6

6 boneless, skinless chicken breasts
1/2 t. kosher salt
1 t. pepper
3 to 4 T. Dijon mustard
2 T. fresh rosemary, minced
2 T. fresh thyme, minced
2 T. fresh parsley, minced

Sprinkle chicken with salt and pepper. Grill over medium-high heat 6 minutes per side, or until juices run clear. Remove from grill and brush both sides with mustard; sprinkle with herbs.

Whole Acorn Squash Cream Soup

Dijon Chicken & Fresh Herbs

Melissa Hart, Middleville, MI

Zucchini Fritters

Here's a tasty way to get your family to eat their vegetables and use the surplus zucchini from your garden! These can be made so quickly and everyone loves them!

Serves 4

2 zucchini, grated (about 3-1/2 c.)
1 egg, beaten
2/3 c. shredded Cheddar cheese
2/3 c. round buttery crackers,
    crumbled
Optional: 1/2 t. seasoned salt
2 T. oil

Combine zucchini, egg, cheese, crackers and, if desired, salt in a large mixing bowl. If mixture seems wet, add extra crackers; shape mixture into patties. Heat oil in a skillet; fry patties about 3 minutes on each side or until golden.

Zucchini Fritters

Jennifer Martineau, Delaware, OH

Gramma's Smothered Swiss Steak

This classic recipe is perfect for any night of the week, but I often serve it for Sunday lunch. I serve it with fresh green beans and roasted potatoes.... what a treat!

Serves 6

1-1/2 lbs. beef round steak, cut into
    serving-size pieces
1 T. oil
1 small onion, halved and sliced
1 carrot, peeled and shredded
1 c. sliced mushrooms
10-3/4 oz. can cream of
    chicken soup
8-oz. can tomato sauce

Brown beef in oil in a skillet over medium heat; drain and set aside. Arrange vegetables in a slow cooker; place beef on top. Mix together soup and tomato sauce; pour over beef and vegetables. Cover and cook on low setting for 6 hours, or until beef is tender.

Gramma's Smothered Swiss Steak

Joan White, Malvern, PA

Simple Scalloped Tomatoes

This tangy-sweet dish makes a delicious dinner. Serve with cheese bread and a fresh green salad for a complete meal.

Serves 4 to 6

1 onion, chopped
1/4 c. butter
28-oz. can diced tomatoes
5 slices bread, lightly toasted and cubed
1/4 c. brown sugar, packed
1/2 t. salt
1/4 t. pepper

Cook onion in butter until just tender, but not browned. Combine onion mixture with tomatoes and their juice in a bowl; add remaining ingredients, and mix well. Pour into a greased 8"x8" baking pan. Bake, uncovered, at 350 degrees for 45 minutes.

Recipe and Photo Courtesy of BeefItsWhatsForDinner.com

Mongolian Beef

You'll love this flavorful dish that is really quite easy to make. Choose the veggie ingredients you like to personalize it for your family.

Serves 4

1 lb. beef top sirloin steak, cut 1-inch thick
2 T. garlic, minced and divided
1/4 to 1/2 t. cayenne pepper
1/2 c. green onions, chopped
1/4 c. oyster sauce
2 T. sugar
1 T. fresh ginger, peeled and choopped
2 c. bamboo shoots, edamame, baby corn or water chestnuts
2 c. hot cooked rice

Cut beef in half lengthwise, then crosswise into 1/8-inch strips. Toss beef with 1 tablespoon garlic and cayenne pepper. Heat non-stick skillet over medium-high heat until hot. Add half of beef; stir-fry one to 2 minutes or until outside surface of beef is no longer pink. Remove from skillet. Repeat with remaining beef. Remove from skillet. Add remaining one tablespoon garlic, green onions, oyster sauce, sugar and ginger to same skillet; cook for one to 2 minutes or until sauce is hot. Return beef to skillet. Add desired vegetable; cook and stir until heated through. Serve over rice.

Mongolian Beef

Karen Puchnick, Butler, PA

Crispy Corn Fritters

So easy to make...delicious with a pasta salad!

Makes 6 to 8 servings

1 c. biscuit baking mix
1/2 c. milk
1 egg, beaten
1 c. frozen corn, thawed
pepper to taste
2 T. oil
Optional: honey

In a bowl, stir together baking mix, milk and egg until just blended. Stir in corn; season with pepper. Let batter stand for 5 to 10 minutes. Heat oil in a skillet over medium heat. Drop batter into oil with a large spoon. Cook until golden; turn and cook one minute on the other side. Drain on paper towels. Serve drizzled with a little honey if desired.

Crispy Corn Fritters

Claudia Olsen, Chester, NJ

Penne & Goat Cheese Salad

One of my husband's favorite pasta dishes...it's just a little different from most. Try arugula for a slightly spicy taste or feta cheese if you prefer it to goat cheese. This makes a great main dish for a light dinner.

Makes 8 servings

12-oz. pkg. penne pasta, uncooked
1 T. garlic, minced
1/4 c. mayonnaise
4-oz. pkg. goat cheese, diced
1/2 c. sun-dried tomatoes packed in
   oil, drained and oil reserved
2 c. baby spinach, coarsely chopped

Cook pasta according to package directions; drain and rinse with cold water. In a large bowl, combine pasta with garlic, mayonnaise and goat cheese. Finely chop tomatoes and add along with spinach; mix gently. Stir in reserved oil from tomatoes, one tablespoon at a time, until ingredients are nicely coated. Serve at room temperature, or cover and chill.

Penne & Goat Cheese Salad

Wendy Reaume, Ontario, Canada

Cheesy Chile Rice

When I was growing up, my mom made this simple rice dish whenever we had Mexican food for dinner. It's yummy with burritos and tortilla chips.

Makes 6 servings

2 c. water
2 c. instant rice, uncooked
16-oz. container sour cream
4-oz. can diced green chiles
3 c. shredded Cheddar cheese, divided

In a saucepan over medium-high heat, bring water to a boil. Stir in rice; remove from heat. Cover and let stand 5 minutes, until water is absorbed. In a large bowl, mix together rice, sour cream, chiles and 2 cups cheese. Spread in a greased 2-quart casserole dish; top with remaining cheese. Bake, uncovered, at 400 degrees for 30 minutes, or until cheese is melted and top is lightly golden.

Brenda Rogers, Atwood, CA

South-of-the-Border Squash Skillet

Our family grows lots of yellow summer squash in our community garden. We love tacos, so this taco-flavored recipe is a yummy way to use it up! If you omit the meat, it's also a great vegetarian dish.

Makes 4 servings

1 lb. ground beef or turkey
1/3 c. onion, diced
1 c. water
1-1/4 oz. pkg. taco seasoning mix
4 to 5 yellow squash, zucchini or crookneck squash, chopped
1 c. shredded Cheddar cheese

In a skillet over medium heat, brown meat with onion; drain. Stir in water and taco seasoning; add squash. Cover and simmer for about 10 minutes, until squash is tender. Stir in cheese; cover and let stand just until cheese melts.

Punch it Up
For a change of pace and a little extra spice, use seasoned ground pork sausage instead of beef or turkey in this skillet recipe. You'll love it!

South-of-the-Border Squash Skillet

Sharon Tillman, Hampton, VA

Sam's Sweet-and-Sour Pork

My best friend Samantha shared this with me. A tasty dish that cooks up in a snap!

Serves 6 to 8

1 T. oil
1 lb. boneless pork loin, cut into
    1/2-inch cubes
1 c. onion, chopped
1 c. green pepper, cut into 3/4-inch
    cubes
1 c. red pepper, cut into 3/4-inch
    cubes
1 t. garlic, minced
8-oz. can pineapple chunks, drained
1 c. catsup
1 T. brown sugar, packed
1 T. white vinegar
1/2 t. salt
1/4 t. pepper
cooked rice

Heat oil in a large skillet over medium heat; brown pork on both sides. Add onion, peppers and garlic; cook and stir 5 minutes. Drain; add remaining ingredients except rice. Cover and simmer 10 minutes, or until pork is tender. Serve over hot rice.

Recipe and Photo Courtesy of BeefItsWhatsForDinner.com

Beefy Harvest Soup

Other pasta shapes, such as rotini, bowties, medium shells or ditalini, may be substituted for large elbow macaroni; adjust cooking time as needed.

Serves 5

1 lb. lean ground beef
2 c. water
14-1/2 oz. can Italian-style stewed
    tomatoes
1-1/2 c. frozen mixed vegetables
4 c. reduced-sodium beef broth
1 c. large elbow macaroni, uncooked
1/4 lb. smoked beef sausage, sliced
salt and pepper to taste

Heat large non-stick skillet over medium heat until hot. Add beef; cook 8 to 10 minutes, breaking into crumbles and stirring occasionally. Remove from skillet with slotted spoon. Remove drippings. Meanwhile, combine water, tomatoes with juice, vegetables and broth in large saucepan; bring to a boil. Stir in macaroni and beef; return to a boil. Reduce heat; simmer, uncovered, 8 minutes, stirring occasionally. Stir in sausage; continue simmering 2 to 4 minutes, or until macaroni is tender and beef sausage is cooked through. Season with salt and pepper, as desired.

Beefy Harvest Soup

Diana Chaney, Olathe, KS

Corn Pudding

The fresh sweet corn in this dish is the secret. Yum!

Serves 6 to 8

9 ears corn
4 eggs, beaten
1/2 c. half-and-half
1-1/2 t. baking powder
1/3 c. butter
2 T. sugar
2 T. all-purpose flour
1 T. butter, melted
1/8 t. pepper

Remove and discard husks and silks from corn. Cut off tips of corn kernels into a bowl; scrape milk and remaining pulp from cob with a paring knife to measure 3 to 4 cups total. Set corn aside. Combine eggs, half-and-half and baking powder, stirring well with a wire whisk. Melt 1/3 cup butter in a large saucepan over low heat; add sugar and flour, stirring until smooth. Remove from heat; gradually add egg mixture, whisking constantly until smooth. Stir in corn. Pour corn mixture into a greased one or 1-1/2 quart casserole dish. Bake, uncovered, at 350 degrees for 40 to 45 minutes, or until pudding is set. Drizzle with melted butter; sprinkle with pepper. Broil 5-1/2 inches from heat 2 minutes or until golden. Let stand 5 minutes before serving.

Joanne Curran, Arlington, MA

Slow-Cooker Country Chicken & Dumplings

Everyone loves chicken and dumplings! Using refrigerated biscuits for the dumplings and a slow cooker to heat makes this recipe a lifesaver on busy weeknights.

Serves 6

4 boneless, skinless chicken breasts, cut into large chunks
1 to 2 T. oil
2 10-3/4 oz. cans cream of chicken soup
2 T. butter, sliced
1 onion, finely diced
1 c. frozen peas
2 7-1/2 oz. tubes refrigerated biscuits, torn
Garnish: chopped parsley

In a skillet over medium heat, brown chicken in oil on all sides; drain. Place chicken, soup, butter and onion in a 4-quart slow cooker; add enough water to cover chicken. Cover and cook on high setting for 4 hours. Add peas and biscuits to slow cooker; gently push biscuits into cooking liquid. Cover and continue cooking for about 1-1/2 hours, until biscuits are done in the center.

Slow-Cooker Country Chicken & Dumplings

Carol Lytle, Columbus, OH

Country Cabin Potatoes

One fall, we stayed in a beautiful 1800s log cabin in southern Ohio. Not only was it peaceful and relaxing, but the meals they served were wonderful! I got this recipe there.

Makes 10 to 12 servings

4 14-1/2 oz. cans sliced potatoes, drained
2 10-3/4 oz. cans cream of celery soup
16-oz. container sour cream
10 slices bacon, crisply cooked and crumbled
6 green onions, thinly sliced

Place potatoes in a slow cooker. In a bowl, combine remaining ingredients; pour over potatoes and stir gently. Cover and cook on high setting for 4 to 5 hours.

Country Cabin Potatoes

Recipe and Photo Courtesy of BeefItsWhatsForDinner.com

Classic Beef Pot Roast

This is a classic dinner that everyone enjoys.

Serves 6

1/2 c. all-purpose flour
1 t. salt
1 t. pepper
2-1/2 to 3-1/2 lb. boneless beef chuck roast or arm roast
1 T. oil
4 c. reduced-sodium beef broth
2 T. tomato paste
2 t. dried thyme
1 lb. new redskin potatoes, cut in half
1 lb. carrots, peeled and cut into 1-1/2 inch pieces
2 large onions, cut into 8 wedges each

Combine flour, salt and pepper; coat beef roast with 2 tablespoons flour mixture. Reserve remaining flour mixture. Heat oil in a stockpot over medium heat until hot. Place roast in stockpot; brown evenly. Pour off drippings. Combine broth, tomato paste and thyme in stockpot; whisk in reserved flour mixture. Bring to a boil. Reduce heat; cover tightly and simmer 1-3/4 to 2 hours. Stir gravy in stockpot. Add potatoes, carrots and onions to stockpot; bring to a boil. Reduce heat; cover tightly and simmer 45 minutes to one hour, until roast and vegetables are fork-tender. Carve roast into slices or chunks; serve with vegetables and gravy.

Classic Beef Pot Roast

Flo Burtnett, Gage, OK

One-Pot Spaghetti

This is a great dinner to make when time is short but everyone is hungry. It fills them up and you don't have to spend a lot of time cleaning up!

Makes 4 servings

1 lb. ground beef
1 onion, diced
2 14-oz. cans chicken broth
6-oz. can tomato paste
1/2 t. dried oregano
1/2 t. salt
1/4 t. pepper
1/8 t. garlic powder
8-oz. pkg. spaghetti, uncooked and
    broken
Garnish: grated Parmesan cheese

Brown ground beef and onion in a large skillet over medium heat. Drain; return to skillet. Stir in broth, tomato paste and seasonings; bring to a boil. Add spaghetti; reduce heat and simmer, stirring often, 15 minutes, or until spaghetti is tender. Sprinkle with cheese.

Jill Valentine, Jackson, TN

Slow-Cooker Butternut Squash Soup

Just chop a few ingredients and combine in the slow cooker for a delicious gourmet soup...so easy!

Serves 8

2-1/2 lbs. butternut squash, peeled,
    halved, seeded and cubed
2 c. leeks, chopped
2 Granny Smith apples, peeled,
    cored and diced
2 14-1/2 oz. cans chicken broth
1 c. water
seasoned salt and white pepper to
    taste
Garnish: freshly ground nutmeg and
    sour cream

Combine squash, leeks, apples, broth and water in a 4-quart slow cooker. Cover and cook on high setting for 4 hours, or until squash and leeks are tender. Carefully purée the hot soup in 3 or 4 batches in a food processor or blender until smooth. Add seasoned salt and white pepper. Garnish with nutmeg and sour cream.

Slow-Cooker Butternut Squash Soup

Cynthia Armstrong, Big Stone Gap, VA

Poor Man's Steak & Vegetables

This recipe has been handed down for several generations. My mother used to serve this dish when money was tight.

Serves 6

6 ground beef patties
4 potatoes, peeled and cubed
3 carrots, peeled and diced
1 onion, quartered or sliced
salt and pepper to taste

Place beef patties in a greased 13"x9" baking pan. Evenly arrange vegetables over patties. Sprinkle with salt and pepper to taste. Bake, covered, at 400 degrees for 45 to 50 minutes, or until beef is no longer pink and potatoes are tender.

Jeanne Barringer, Edgewater, FL

Sour Cream Mini Biscuits

Once you start snacking on these, it's hard to stop!

Makes 4 dozen

1 c. butter, softened
1 c. sour cream
2 c. self-rising flour

Blend butter and sour cream together until fluffy; gradually mix in flour. Drop by teaspoonfuls into greased mini muffin tins; bake at 450 degrees for 10 to 12 minutes.

Cheri Maxwell, Gulf Breeze, FL

Broccoli Quiche Peppers

We love these colorful peppers for a dinner that's just a little different.

Makes 4 servings

4 red, yellow or green peppers, tops
    cut off and reserved
4 eggs, beaten
1/2 c. milk
1 c. broccoli, finely chopped
1/2 t. garlic powder
1/4 t. Italian seasoning
Optional: shredded mozzarella
    cheese

Finely dice reserved tops of peppers; set aside. Place pepper shells upright in custard cups; set cups in a 9"x9" baking pan. In a bowl, whisk together eggs, milk, broccoli, diced pepper and seasonings; pour evenly into peppers. Bake, uncovered, at 325 degrees for 40 to 50 minutes, until peppers are tender and egg mixture is set. Top with cheese if desired and bake 10 more minutes. Let stand 5 minutes before serving.

Broccoli Quiche Peppers

Jodi Zarnoth-Hirsch, Chilton, WI

Cranberry Meatloaves

This favorite comfort food recipe is dressed up with a yummy cranberry topping.

Serves 5

1 lb. lean ground beef
1 c. cooked rice
1/2 c. tomato juice
1/4 c. onion, minced
1 egg
1 t. salt
16-oz. can whole-berry cranberry
    sauce
1/3 c. brown sugar, packed
1 T. lemon juice

Mix together ground beef, rice, tomato juice, onion, egg and salt. Shape mixture evenly into 5 mini meatloaves and place in a greased 13"x9" baking pan. Mix together cranberry sauce, brown sugar and lemon juice; spoon over top of each loaf. Bake at 350 degrees for 45 minutes.

Sharon Demers, Dolores, CO

Firecracker Grilled Salmon

Add more red pepper flakes or a dusting of cayenne pepper for even more heat!

Serves 4

4 4 to 6-oz. salmon fillets
1/4 c. peanut oil
2 T. soy sauce
2 T. balsamic vinegar
2 T. green onions, chopped
1-1/2 t. brown sugar, packed
1 clove garlic, minced
1/2 t. red pepper flakes
1/2 t. sesame oil
1/8 t. salt

Place salmon in a glass baking pan. Whisk together remaining ingredients and pour over salmon. Cover with plastic wrap; refrigerate 4 to 6 hours. Remove salmon, discarding marinade. Place on an aluminum foil-lined grill that has been sprayed with non-stick vegetable spray. Grill 10 minutes per inch of thickness, measured at thickest part, until fish flakes easily with a fork. Turn halfway through cooking.

Firecracker Grilled Salmon

Donna Harpster, Kansas City, MO

Green Peas with Crispy Bacon

Rather than chase little round peas around the plate, be sure to serve this side with biscuits, or "pea pushers," to help you get every pea on your fork.

Serves 6

2 slices bacon
1 shallot, sliced
1/2 t. orange zest
1/2 c. fresh orange juice
1/2 t. pepper
1/4 t. salt
16-oz. pkg. frozen sweet green peas, thawed
1 t. butter
1 T. fresh mint, chopped
Garnish: fresh mint sprig

Cook bacon in a skillet over medium heat until crisp; remove and drain on paper towels, reserving one teaspoon drippings in skillet. Crumble bacon and set aside. Sauté shallot in hot bacon drippings over medium-high heat 2 minutes or until tender. Stir in orange zest, orange juice, pepper and salt. Cook, stirring occasionally, 5 minutes or until reduced by half. Add peas and cook 5 more minutes; stir in butter and chopped mint. Transfer peas to a serving dish and sprinkle with crumbled bacon. Garnish, if desired.

Karla Neese, Edmond, OK

Savory Herb Roast

My mom would always put this roast into the slow cooker early on Sunday mornings, before getting ready for church. When we came home from church around noon, the whole house smelled wonderful! Now I make it for a special weeknight dinner!

Serves 6

3-lb. boneless beef chuck roast
salt and pepper to taste
1 to 2 T. oil
1 T. fresh chives, chopped
1 T. fresh parsley, chopped
1 T. fresh basil, chopped
1 c. beef broth
Optional: 4 to 6 potatoes, peeled and quartered; 3 to 4 carrots, peeled and cut into chunks

Sprinkle roast generously with salt and pepper. Heat oil in a skillet; add herbs. Brown roast on all sides. Place in slow cooker; add broth. Cover and cook on low setting for 6 to 8 hours. Add potatoes and carrots during the last 2 hours of cooking if desired.

Savory Herb Roast

Tammi Miller, Attleboro, MA

Apple Spice Country Ribs

One fall weekend after apple picking, I tossed together this recipe. I was trying to work apples into everything I could think of to use them up, and I used some of the last ones in this slow-cooker recipe. Serve with mashed potatoes or cooked rice.

Serves 6

2 to 3 lbs. boneless country pork ribs
3 baking apples, cored and cut into
    wedges
1 onion, thinly sliced
2/3 c. apple cider
1 t. cinnamon
1 t. allspice
1/2 t. salt
1/4 t. pepper

Place all ingredients in a 5-quart slow cooker; stir to coat. Cover and cook on low setting for 7 to 9 hours. Juices will thicken as they cool; stir if separated. Serve with mashed potatoes or hot cooked rice if desired. (If bone-in ribs are used, slice into serving-size portions.)

Apple Spice Country Ribs

Eleanor Dionne, Beverly, MA

Ricotta Gnocchi

This is my mother's recipe from more than forty years ago. She made all her pasta by hand. My children look forward to these each time I make it. Now my daughter has learned how to make these and my grandchildren can't wait to eat them. Very easy to do!

Serves 6

32-oz. container ricotta cheese
1 egg, beaten
1 t. salt
4 c. all-purpose flour, divided
Garnish: tomato sauce, grated
    Parmesan cheese

Combine ricotta, egg and salt in a large bowl; mix thoroughly with a large spoon. Gradually add flour, one cup at a time. When dough is no longer sticky, knead slightly on a lightly floured board. Break off chunks; roll into long ropes. Cut ropes into pieces the size of a cherry. Roll in a little flour with the back of a fork. Place on a clean tea towel to dry. To serve gnocchi, boil for 8 to 10 minutes in a large pot of salted water. Garnish with warmed tomato sauce and Parmesan cheese.

Ricotta Gnocchi

Jen Stout, Blandon, PA

Spicy Roasted Potatoes

Mmm...potatoes seasoned with two kinds of mustard! This is a yummy, easy side dish. You don't even need to peel the potatoes.

Makes 4 servings

2 baking potatoes, cut into 1-inch cubes
1-1/2 t. dry mustard
1-1/2 t. Dijon mustard
1 t. olive oil
1 clove garlic, minced
1 T. fresh tarragon, chopped
1/4 t. paprika
1/8 t. cayenne pepper

Place potatoes in a bowl; set aside. In a separate bowl, combine remaining ingredients; stir well and pour over potatoes. Toss potatoes until well coated. Arrange potatoes in a single layer on a lightly greased baking sheet. Bake, uncovered, at 425 degrees for 30 to 35 minutes, until tender and golden.

Spicy Roasted Potatoes

Vickie, Gooseberry Patch

Creamy Bacon & Herb Succotash

You'll love this deluxe version of an old harvest-time favorite...I do!

Serves 6

1/4 lb. bacon, chopped
1 onion, diced
10-oz. pkg. frozen lima beans
1/2 c. water
salt and pepper to taste
10-oz. pkg. frozen corn
1/2 c. whipping cream
1-1/2 t. fresh thyme, minced
Garnish: 2 t. fresh chives, snipped

Cook bacon until crisp in a Dutch oven over medium-high heat. Remove bacon, reserving about 2 tablespoons drippings in Dutch oven. Add onion; sauté about 5 minutes, or until tender. Add beans, water, salt and pepper; bring to a boil. Reduce heat; cover and simmer 5 minutes. Stir in corn, whipping cream and thyme; return to a simmer. Cook until vegetables are tender, about 5 minutes. Toss with bacon and chives before serving.

Creamy Bacon & Herb Succotash

Mignonne Gardner, Pleasant Grove, UT

Slow-Cooker Steak Chili

All summer I long for cool, crisp autumn nights. I created this recipe just for those fabulous fall nights. The aroma of chili fills my home while it simmers.

Makes 8 servings

2 lbs. beef round steak, cut into
 1-inch cubes
1-1/2 c. onion, chopped
2 cloves garlic, minced
2 T. oil
1-1/3 c. water, divided
2 15-oz. cans kidney beans, drained
 and rinsed
2 14-1/2 oz. cans diced tomatoes
16-oz. jar salsa
15-oz. can tomato sauce
1 c. celery, chopped
1-1/2 T. chili powder
1 t. ground cumin
1 t. dried oregano
1/2 t. pepper
2 T. all-purpose flour
2 T. cornmeal
Garnish: shredded Cheddar cheese,
 sour cream, crushed tortilla
 chips

Brown beef, onion and garlic in oil in a large skillet over medium heat; drain. Add beef mixture to a 5-quart slow cooker. Stir in one cup water and remaining ingredients except flour, cornmeal and garnish; mix well. Cover and cook on low setting for 8 hours. Combine flour, cornmeal and remaining 1/3 cup water in a small bowl, whisking until smooth. Add mixture to simmering chili right before serving; stir 2 minutes, or until thickened. Garnish as desired.

Savvy Side
Cornbread loves chili! If you like sweet cornbread, you'll love this family-size recipe. Mix together an 8-1/2 ounce box of corn muffin mix, a 9-ounce box of yellow cake mix, 1/2 cup water, 1/3 cup milk and 2 beaten eggs. Pour into a greased 13"x9" baking pan and bake at 350 degrees for 15 to 20 minutes. Scrumptious!

Slow-Cooker Steak Chili

Tiny Taco Beef

CHAPTER FIVE

Nibbles & Sips

Whether you're having a special party or just need a little snack to get you to the next meal, you'll find that these tasty appetizers and cool drinks are the perfect goodie for you.

Spicy Hummus, Page 206

Raspberry Punch, Page 204

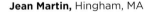

Rosie Jones, Wabash, IN

Raspberry Punch

For toasting a festive occasion, replace the cider with sparkling white wine.

Makes 8 servings

2 c. apple cider
3 c. cranberry-raspberry juice
  cocktail
1 qt. lemonade
Optional: 1 lemon, thinly sliced,
  fresh mint leaves, fresh
  raspberries

Combine apple cider, cranberry-raspberry juice and lemonade in a large pitcher or punch bowl. If desired, garnish glasses with lemon slices, fresh mint leaves or raspberries.

Raspberry Punch

Jean Martin, Hingham, MA

Cheddar-Chive Bites

These little cheesy gems are always a hit at our card parties. Using biscuit mix makes them so easy. Sometimes I add just a little shaved ham along with the cucumber and radishes and everyone seems to love those as well.

Makes 2 to 3 dozen

2-1/2 c. biscuit baking mix
1 c. shredded Cheddar cheese
3/4 c. milk
1/8 t. garlic powder
6 T. butter, melted and divided
3 T. fresh chives, snipped and
  divided
2 5-oz. containers garlic & herb
  cheese spread, softened
Garnish: thinly sliced cucumber and
  radish

Combine baking mix, cheese, milk, garlic powder and 2 tablespoons butter; mix well. Drop by tablespoonfuls onto ungreased baking sheets. Bake at 400 degrees for 10 to 12 minutes, just until golden. Mix remaining butter and one tablespoon chives; brush over warm biscuits. Split biscuits; set aside. Blend cheese spread and remaining chives. Spread lightly onto bottom halves of biscuits; add cucumber, radish and top halves.

Cheddar-Chive Bites

Jo Ann, Gooseberry Patch

Pecan-Stuffed Deviled Eggs

Top with fresh parsley sprigs and chopped pecans for a festive presentation.

Serves 6

6 eggs, hard-boiled and peeled
1/4 c. mayonnaise
1 t. onion, grated
1/2 t. fresh parsley, chopped
1/2 t. dry mustard
1/8 t. salt
1/3 c. pecans, coarsely chopped
Garnish: fresh parsley

Cut eggs in half lengthwise and carefully remove yolks. Mash yolks in a small bowl. Stir in mayonnaise and next 4 ingredients; blend well. Stir in pecans. Spoon or pipe yolk mixture evenly into egg-white halves. Garnish if desired.

Pecan-Stuffed Deviled Eggs

Lizzy Burnley, Ankeny, IA

Spicy Hummus

Using canned beans makes this hummus fast and easy to make.

Serves 10

2 c. canned garbanzo beans, rinsed
    and drained
2 cloves garlic, finely minced
1 t. jalapeño pepper, minced
1/2 t. salt
1/2 t. pepper
3 t. lemon juice
3 t. tahini
3 t. olive oil
1/2 to 1 c. tomato juice
chopped black olives
coarsely chopped tomato

Place garbanzo beans in a food processor. Cover and process until blended. Add garlic, jalapeño pepper, salt and pepper. Cover and process until combined. Add lemon juice, tahini and olive oil. Cover and process until well blended. Mixture will be thick. With machine running, slowly add enough tomato juice to make mixture the desired consistency. Transfer to a serving bowl. If desired, garnish with olives and tomato.

Flavor Fun

Hummus is fun to make because it can be flavored in so many different ways. Try onion powder, dried basil, dried oregano, chopped fresh dill or lemon pepper in place of the jalapeño pepper. Or stir in some chopped black olives, sliced green onion or chopped fresh tomato.

Spicy Hummus

Cinde Shields, Issaquah, WA

Cheesy Spinach-Stuffed Mushrooms

These warm, savory, bite-size beauties always seem to find their way onto my appetizer menu. Everyone loves these little treats!

Makes about 8 servings

10-oz. pkg. frozen chopped spinach, thawed and squeezed dry
1/4 c. cream cheese, softened
1 c. crumbled feta cheese
3/4 t. garlic powder
1/4 t. pepper
24 mushrooms, stems removed
1 c. grated Parmesan cheese

In a bowl, combine all ingredients except mushroom caps and Parmesan cheese; mix well. Spoon mixture into mushrooms; place on a rimmed baking sheet. Sprinkle mushrooms with Parmesan cheese. Bake at 350 degrees for about 15 to 20 minutes, until bubbly and heated through. Serve warm.

Cheesy Spinach-Stuffed Mushrooms

Henry Burnley, Ankeny, IA

Mini Pizzas

Even the kids can help make these little snack pizzas. The crust is a baking powder crust so no rising necessary.

Makes one dozen

1-1/2 c. all-purpose flour
3/4 c. cornmeal
2 T. sugar
1/2 t. baking powder
1/2 t. salt
1 egg, beaten
1/4 c. water
2 T. olive oil
3/4 c. pizza sauce
1/2 c. mini pepperoni slices
1-1/2 c. finely shredded mozzarella or Italian-blend cheese

In a small bowl, mix flour, cornmeal, sugar, baking powder and salt. In another small bowl, beat together egg, water, and oil. Add egg mixture to flour mixture and mix well. Add more water if necessary to form a ball. Divide dough into 12 pieces; form into balls and place on greased baking sheets. Using your fingers, press each ball of dough into a round flat shape. Spread each crust with one tablespoon pizza sauce. Top with pepperoni. Sprinkle with 2 tablespoons cheese. Bake at 375 degrees for about 10 minutes. Increase oven temperature to 400 degrees. Bake about 10 minutes more or until crust begins to brown and cheese is melted and golden.

Mini Pizzas

Elijah Dahlstrom, Ames, IA

Cheese Quesadillas

These easy-to-make little wedges will satisfy everyone at your party!

Serves 8

1-1/2 c. shredded Cheddar cheese
1/4 c. red pepper, chopped
1/4 c. green pepper, chopped
1/4 c. jalapeño peppers, chopped
1 T. olive oil
6 corn tortillas
Garnish: salsa

In a small bowl, combine cheese, sweet peppers and jalapeño peppers. Set aside. In a large skillet, heat oil over medium heat. Place one tortilla in the pan. Spoon 1/3 of the cheese mixture onto tortilla. Place another tortilla on top of cheese mixture. Press lightly. Cook until cheese is melted and tortillas are crisp and golden, turning with a spatula to cook both sides. Remove from skillet. Make 2 more quesadillas. Cut quesadillas into wedges. Serve with salsa.

Lynda McCormick, Burkburnett, TX

Greek Pita Pizza

These pizzas are so deep and rich in color and they are very nutritious as well.

Makes 8 servings

10-oz. pkg. frozen chopped spinach, thawed and well drained
4 green onions, chopped
1 T. fresh dill, chopped
garlic salt and pepper to taste
4 whole-wheat pita rounds, split
4 roma tomatoes, sliced 1/2-inch thick
1/2 c. crumbled feta cheese with basil & tomato
dried oregano or Greek seasoning to taste

Mix spinach, onions and dill in a small bowl. Season with garlic salt and pepper; set aside. Place pita rounds on ungreased baking sheets. Arrange tomato slices among pitas. Spread spinach mixture evenly over tomatoes; spread cheese over tomatoes. Sprinkle with desired seasoning. Bake at 450 degrees for 10 to 15 minutes, until crisp. Cut into wedges.

Cheese Quesadillas

Greek Pita Pizza

NIBBLES & SIPS

Katie Majeske, Denver, PA

Island Chiller

So delicious, especially in the summertime. And it's only 68 calories per serving.

Makes 8 servings

10-oz. pkg. frozen strawberries
15-oz. can crushed pineapple
1-1/2 c. orange juice
1-qt. bottle club soda or sparkling
　　water, chilled
Garnish: strawberries

In a blender, combine frozen strawberries, pineapple with juice and orange juice. Blend until smooth and frothy. Pour mixture into ice cube trays and freeze. To serve, put 3 cubes into each of 8 tall glasses; add 1/2 cup club soda or sparkling water to each glass. Let stand until mixture becomes slushy. Garnish each glass with a strawberry, as desired.

Barb Bargdill, Gooseberry Patch

Cheesy Tuna Melts

It's the sweet raisin bread and chopped apple that make these sandwiches stand out from all the rest.

Makes 12 servings

1 T. oil
1 c. apple, cored and chopped
3 T. onion, chopped
7-oz. can albacore tuna, drained
1/4 c. chopped walnuts
1/4 c. light mayonnaise
2 t. lemon juice
1/8 t. salt
1/8 t. pepper
6 slices raisin bread, toasted and
　　halved diagonally
6 slices sharp Cheddar cheese,
　　halved diagonally

Heat oil in a skillet over medium heat; add apple and onion. Cook, stirring occasionally, about 5 minutes, until tender. Remove from heat; transfer to a bowl. Stir in tuna, walnuts, mayonnaise, lemon juice, salt and pepper. Place toast slices on an ungreased baking sheet. Top with tuna mixture and a slice of cheese. Broil 4 to 5 inches from heat for 3 to 4 minutes, or until cheese begins to melt.

Island Chiller

Cheesy Tuna Melts

Erin Brock, Charleston, WV

Pinwheel Starters

Use spinach tortillas to add color to these tasty little appetizers.

Serves 16

8-oz. pkg. low-fat cream cheese,
   softened
2 T. light ranch salad dressing
3 12-inch wheat or spinach tortillas
3/4 c. Kalamata olives, chopped
1 c. carrots, peeled and shredded

Mix together cream cheese and ranch dressing. Spread cream cheese mixture evenly over one side of each tortilla. Stir together olives and carrots. Spoon over cream cheese mixture. Roll up each tortilla jelly-roll style; wrap each in plastic wrap. Chill for at least 2 hours; cut into one-inch slices.

Diane Stevenson, Marion, IA

Yummy Snack Mix

A wonderful blend of flavors and textures makes this snack mix a great addition to any party.

Serves 20

2 c. bite-size crispy corn cereal
2 c. bite-size crispy rice cereal
2 c. round corn cereal
1/2 c. whole cashews
1/2 c. whole almonds
1/2 c. raisins
1/2 c. dried apricots, chopped
1/2 c. butter, melted
1/2 c. sugar
1 t. cinnamon

In a large bowl, combine cereals, cashews, almonds, raisins and apricots. Pour melted butter over mixture and toss lightly. In a separate bowl, mix together sugar and cinnamon; sprinkle over cereal mixture. Mix well. Pour into a large shallow baking pan. Bake at 250 degrees for 1 hour, stirring every 15 minutes. Cool.

Yummy Snack Mix

Zoe Bennett, Columbia, SC

Tangy Radish Bites

These beautiful little finger sandwiches will be the talk of the party. My friends just love them!

Makes 16 servings

2 T. butter, softened
3 T. fresh chives, chopped
1 T. toasted sesame seed
3/4 t. fresh ginger, peeled and grated
1/4 t. sesame oil
1/8 t. salt
1/8 t. pepper
1 whole-grain baguette, sliced
　1/4-inch thick
10 radishes, thinly sliced
Garnish: edible flowers, pea sprouts

Mix butter, chives, sesame seed, ginger and oil in a bowl. Add salt and pepper and mix well. Spread mixture over one side of each baguette slice. Top with radishes, overlapping slightly. Garnish as desired.

Recipe and Photo Courtesy of
BeefItsWhatsForDinner.com

Tiny Taco Beef

These tasty, tiny tacos will disappear fast!

Serves 15

12 oz. lean ground beef
1/2 c. onion, chopped
1 t. garlic, minced
1/2 c. taco sauce
1/2 t. ground cumin
1/4 t. salt
1/8 t. pepper
2 2.1-oz. pkgs. frozen mini phyllo
　shells (30 shells total)
1/2 c. shredded Mexican cheese
　blend
Garnish: shredded lettuce, sliced
　grape tomatoes, guacamole, sour
　cream, sliced black olives

Heat a large non-stick skillet over medium heat until hot. Add beef, onion and garlic to skillet. Cook over medium heat 8 to 10 minutes, breaking up beef into small crumbles and stirring occasionally. Add taco sauce, cumin, salt and pepper; cook and stir one to 2 minutes or until mixture is heated through. Place phyllo shells on a rimmed baking sheet. Spoon beef mixture evenly into shells. Top evenly with cheese. Bake at 350 degrees for 9 to 10 minutes, until shells are crisp and cheese is melted. Garnish as desired.

Tiny Taco Beef

Charlotte Harding, Starkville, MS

Summertime Iced Tea

You can enjoy this refreshing drink any time of year...in the summertime it really hits the spot!

Makes 10 servings

4 c. boiling water
2 family-size tea bags
6 leaves fresh mint
6-oz. can frozen lemonade
  concentrate
1 c. sugar
5 c. cold water
ice cubes
Garnish: fresh mint sprigs

Pour boiling water into a large heatproof pitcher. Add tea bags and mint leaves; let stand for 5 minutes. Discard tea bags and mint leaves. Add frozen lemonade, sugar and cold water, mixing well. Serve over ice; garnish with mint sprigs.

Andrew Neymeyer, Des Moines, IA

Pepperoni Pizza Sandwiches

This recipe could not be any easier, or more delicious!

Serves 6

3 bagels, halved
5-oz. pkg. mini pepperoni slices
8-oz. pkg. shredded Italian-style
  shredded cheese
1 c. pizza sauce

Lay bagel halves cut-side up on a baking sheet. Spread a thin layer of pizza sauce on each bagel. Sprinkle a layer of cheese on the sauce. Top with slices of pepperoni. Top with more cheese, if desired. Bake at 375 degrees for about 10 minutes, until cheese is melted. Serve immediately.

Summertime Iced Tea

Pepperoni Pizza Sandwiches

Lisa McClelland, Columbus, OH

Cucumber-Lime Agua Fresca

On a trip to Mexico, I was served this beverage one hot day. It's very refreshing...a great way to use up cucumbers and mint! The lime adds the tartness.

Makes 4 servings

1 lb. cucumbers, cubed
6 c. water, divided
1/4 c. fresh mint, chopped
2 T. sugar
2 T. lime juice
ice cubes
Garnish: lime slices, cucumber
   slices

Combine cucumbers, 2 cups water and mint in a blender. Process until puréed. Let stand in blender for 5 minutes to steep. Strain into a 2-quart pitcher. Add remaining water, sugar, lime juice and ice. Stir to combine; add more sugar, if desired. Divide evenly into 4 tall glasses; garnish as desired. Serve immediately.

Margaret Collins, Clarendon Hills, IL

Chicken-Salsa Dip

This recipe becomes dinner when I add a fresh fruit salad and some cookies and ice cream for dessert!

Serves 8

8-oz. jar salsa, divided
8-oz. pkg. cream cheese, softened
8-oz. pkg. shredded Mexican-blend
   cheese
2 to 3 boneless, skinless chicken
   breasts, cooked and diced

Blend half the salsa with the cream cheese; spread on the bottom of an ungreased 9" pie plate. Top with remaining salsa; sprinkle with cheese and chicken. Bake at 350 degrees for 25 minutes.

Chicken-Salsa Dip

Anna McMaster, Portland, OR

Cucumber & Salmon Rounds

The rich salmon mixture also makes a great sandwich spread.

Serves 12

3-oz. cooked salmon fillet
1 t. lemon juice
1 t. fresh dill, chopped
1/2 c. plain Greek yogurt
3 whole cucumbers
Garnish: fresh dill or parsley sprigs

Blend salmon, lemon juice, dill and yogurt. Place in a covered container and chill one hour. Make a design on the outside of the whole cucumbers by slicing several thin strips of peel from the length of the cucumber, or scoring the peel with the tines of a fork. Cut into 1/8-inch slices. Spread with chilled salmon mixture and garnish with dill or parsley.

Wendy Lee Paffenroth, Pine Island, NY

Market Veggie Triangles

These little triangle sandwiches arrange so nicely on an appetizer tray. Enjoy!

Serves 24

3 cucumbers, chopped
8-oz. pkg. low-fat cream cheese, softened
1/4 c. mayonnaise
1 T. lemon juice
1/8 t. hot pepper sauce
1/2 c. red pepper, chopped
1/4 c. onion, finely chopped
1/4 c. green olives with pimentos, finely chopped
1 T. fresh parsley, chopped
1/2 t. pepper
12 slices pumpernickel bread, crusts trimmed
Garnish: sliced green olives

Place cucumbers in a strainer for 15 to 20 minutes to allow liquid to drain. Combine remaining ingredients except bread and garnish in a bowl. Stir until well blended. Add drained cucumbers; stir again. Refrigerate, covered, for 2 to 3 hours. Slice bread into triangles. Spread with cucumber mixture. Garnish as desired.

Market Veggie Triangles

Gram's Zucchini Cookies

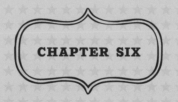

CHAPTER SIX

Relax with Dessert

There is always room for dessert! You will love these recipes that make your sweet tooth very happy.

Grandmother's Waffle Cookies, Page 234   Royal Strawberry Shortcake, Page 244

Janis Parr, Ontario, Canada

Can't-Be-Beet Cake

No one would guess this moist and delicious cake has beets and carrots in it! Even the kids love it!

Makes 16 servings

3 eggs, separated
1/3 c. canola oil
1 c. sugar
3 T. hot water
2 c. all-purpose flour
2-1/2 t. baking powder
1 t. cinnamon
1 t. vanilla extract
1/2 c. chopped pecans
1 c. beets, peeled and grated
1 c. carrots, peeled and grated
Garnish: thin frosting

In a deep bowl, beat egg whites with an electric mixer on high speed until stiff peaks form; set aside. In a separate large bowl, combine egg yolks and remaining ingredients except garnish. Mix well; fold in the egg whites. Pour batter into a greased and floured 12"x8" baking pan. Bake at 350 degrees for 35 minutes, or until a toothpick inserted in the center tests done. Cool before slicing. Garnish as desired.

Nancy Willis, Farmington Hills, MI

Easy Apple Crisp

Garnish with a dollop of whipped cream and a dusting of cinnamon or an apple slice.

Serves 12

4 c. apples, cored and sliced
1/2 c. brown sugar, packed
1/2 c. quick-cooking oats, uncooked
1/3 c. all-purpose flour
3/4 t. cinnamon
1/4 c. butter
Garnish: whipped cream, cinnamon, apple slice

Arrange apple slices in a greased 11"x8" baking pan; set aside. Combine remaining ingredients; stir until crumbly and sprinkle over apples. Bake at 350 degrees for 30 to 35 minutes. Garnish as desired.

Good Choice
Granny Smith and Honeycrisp varieties are popular apples to use in apple pies and apple crisps. Golden Delicious is another great choice for a crisp. You can use just one kind of apple, or for added flavor use an assortment of varieties.

Easy Apple Crisp

Barb Lueck, Lester Prairie, MN

Peach Melba Pie

I got this recipe from my mom. It is our favorite summer pie and always makes us look forward to the warm days.

Serves 6

4 peaches, peeled, pitted and sliced
1 c. sugar
5 t. lemon juice
1/4 c. cornstarch
1/3 c. water
3 c. fresh raspberries
9-inch pie crust, baked

In a large saucepan over medium heat, combine peaches, sugar and lemon juice. In a small bowl, stir cornstarch and water until smooth; stir into peach mixture. Bring to a boil; cook and stir one minute, or until thickened. Remove from heat; cool to room temperature. Gently fold in raspberries; spoon into baked pie crust. Chill at least 3 hours to overnight.

Vickie, Gooseberry Patch

Homemade Carrot Cake

This moist and rich carrot cake has just the right amount of spice and the nuts add the perfect texture. Your family will love it!

Serves 18

4 eggs, beaten
3/4 c. canola oil
1/2 c. applesauce
1 c. sugar
1 c. brown sugar, packed
1 T. vanilla extract
2 c. all-purpose flour
2 t. baking powder
2 t. baking soda
1/2 t. salt
1 T. cinnamon
1/2 t. nutmeg
3 c. carrots, peeled and grated
Optional: 1/2 c. chopped pecans
Garnish: carrot curls

In a large bowl, beat together eggs, oil, applesauce, sugars and vanilla. Add remaining ingredients except carrots and pecans; mix well. Stir in carrots; fold in pecans if using. Pour into a greased 13"x9" baking pan. Bake at 350 degrees for 40 to 50 minutes, until a toothpick inserted in center comes out clean. Let cool in pan for 10 minutes; turn out onto a wire rack and cool completely. Frost; garnish with carrot curls.

FROSTING
1/4 c. butter, softened
8-oz. pkg. cream cheese, softened
2 c. powdered sugar
1 t. vanilla extract

Combine all ingredients in a bowl. Beat until smooth and creamy.

Homemade Carrot Cake

Gail Kelsey, Phoenix, AZ

Blue-Ribbon Pecan Pie

This pie has won a blue ribbon at our state fair every time I entered it! It's a family favorite and is always a part of our Christmas dinner.

Serves 8

9-inch pie crust, unbaked
1/2 c. pecan halves
3 eggs
1 c. dark corn syrup
1 c. sugar
1 t. vanilla extract
1/8 t. salt

Place unbaked crust in a 9" pie plate. Arrange pecans in crust; set aside. In a bowl, beat eggs well. Add remaining ingredients; mix well. Pour mixture over pecans in crust. Bake at 400 degrees for 15 minutes; reduce oven to 325 degrees. Bake an additional 30 minutes, or until center of pie is set. Cool completely.

Jo Ann, Gooseberry Patch

Chocolate Cappuccino Brownies

Chewy and chocolatey together, with a touch of coffee flavor...delicious!

Makes 1-1/2 to 2 dozen

1/2 c. butter, melted
1 c. brown sugar, packed
2 T. instant coffee granules
3 eggs, slightly beaten
1 t. vanilla extract
1/2 c. brewed coffee, cooled
1 t. baking powder
1/2 t. salt
1-1/4 c. all-purpose flour, sifted
1/3 c. plus 1 T. baking cocoa
1 c. chopped walnuts
1 c. semi-sweet chocolate chips
Garnish: powdered sugar

In a bowl, combine butter, brown sugar and coffee granules; blend well. Add eggs, vanilla and cooled coffee; stir. In a separate bowl, combine baking powder, salt, flour and cocoa; add to butter mixture. Stir in walnuts and chocolate chips, mixing well. Pour batter into a greased 13"x9" baking pan. Bake at 350 degrees for 25 to 30 minutes. Allow brownies to cool. Cut into squares. Dust with powdered sugar before serving.

Chocolate Cappuccino Brownies

Carole Akers, Bellevue, OH

Butter Pecan Peach Cake

So refreshing in the summer, or serve warm on chilly days...a yummy treat either way!

Serves 18 to 24

29-oz. can sliced peaches
18-1/4 oz. pkg. butter pecan or yellow
  cake mix
1/2 c. butter, melted
1 c. chopped pecans
1 c. sweetened flaked coconut

Pour sliced peaches and syrup in the bottom of an ungreased 13"x9" baking pan. Cover with dry cake mix; drizzle butter over the top. Sprinkle with pecans and coconut. Bake, uncovered, at 350 degrees for 30 to 35 minutes.

Jennie Gist, Gooseberry Patch

Apple Bread Pudding

Day-old bread is best for soaking up the liquid in this oh-so-decadent dessert.

Serves 12

4 eggs
1-1/2 c. sugar
3 12-oz. cans evaporated milk
1/2 c. butter, melted

1 T. vanilla extract
2 t. cinnamon
6 c. French bread, torn into pieces
  and packed
1 Granny Smith apple, peeled, cored
  and chopped
1-1/2 c. walnuts, coarsely chopped
  and toasted
1 c. golden raisins

Whisk eggs in a large bowl. Whisk in sugar, evaporated milk, melted butter, vanilla and cinnamon. Fold in bread and remaining ingredients, stirring until bread is moistened. Pour into a greased 13"x9" baking pan. Bake, uncovered, at 350 degrees for 50 minutes or until set. Cut into squares. Serve warm with Rum Sauce.

RUM SAUCE
2 14-oz. cans sweetened condensed
  milk
2 T. dark rum or 1 t. rum extract
1 T. vanilla extract

Pour condensed milk into a small saucepan; cook over medium heat until hot, stirring often. Remove from heat; stir in rum and vanilla. Serve warm. Makes 2-1/2 cups.

Apple Bread Pudding

Trudy Cox, Plano, TX

The Best Oatmeal Cookies

The name of this recipe says it all! This is a recipe I received from a friend back in 1989.

Makes 4 dozen

1 c. golden raisins
3 eggs, beaten
1 t. vanilla extract
1 c. butter, softened
1 c. brown sugar, packed
1 c. sugar
2-1/2 c. all-purpose flour
1 t. salt
2 t. baking soda
1 T. cinnamon
2 c. quick-cooking oats, uncooked
1 c. chopped pecans

In a small bowl, combine raisins, eggs and vanilla. Cover with plastic wrap and let stand one hour. In a large bowl, combine butter and sugars. In a separate bowl, whisk together flour, salt, baking soda and cinnamon. Add flour mixture to butter mixture; mix until well blended. Stir in raisin mixture, oats and pecans. Dough will be stiff. Drop by rounded teaspoonfuls onto ungreased baking sheets. Bake at 350 degrees for 10 to 12 minutes.

Shannon Sitko, Warren, OH

Grandmother's Waffle Cookies

My Grandmother Blanche always made these delicious cookies...we loved them then and we still do!

Makes 3 dozen

1 c. butter, melted and slightly cooled
4 eggs, beaten
1 c. sugar
1 c. brown sugar, packed
2 t. vanilla extract
4 c. all-purpose flour
Optional: frosting and sprinkles

Mix together melted butter, eggs and sugars; add vanilla. Slowly stir in flour. Drop batter by teaspoonfuls onto a preheated ungreased waffle iron. Check cookies after about one minute. Cookies are done when they are a medium golden in center and light golden at the edges. Dip in frosting and sprinkles if desired.

Grandmother's Waffle Cookies

Shelley Turner, Boise, ID

Eva's Fruit Cobbler

This browns so nicely when baked in a cast-iron skillet.

Makes 8 servings

4 c. rhubarb, sliced
4 c. strawberries, hulled and halved
1 c. sugar, divided
1/4 c. water
2 T. apple juice
1 T. cornstarch
1 c. all-purpose flour
1 t. baking powder
1/4 t. baking soda
1/4 t. salt
1/4 c. butter
1/2 c. buttermilk
1/2 t. almond extract
Garnish: 2 t. coarse sugar

In a large, oven-safe skillet, combine fruit, 3/4 cup sugar and water; bring to a boil. Reduce heat, cover and simmer for 10 minutes. Combine apple juice and cornstarch in a container with a tight-fitting lid; shake well to blend. Stir into fruit and cook until mixture thickens. Keep warm. Combine remaining dry ingredients, including remaining sugar, in a bowl. Cut in butter with a pastry blender or 2 forks until mixture resembles crumbs. Stir together buttermilk and extract; add to dough. Stir to blend well and drop by tablespoonfuls onto hot fruit. Sprinkle with coarse sugar. Bake at 400 degrees for 20 minutes, or until golden.

Mary Lou Thomas, Portland, ME

Pineapple Upside-Down Cupcakes

These little gems of sweetness are just as pretty as they are yummy!

Makes one dozen

20-oz. can pineapple tidbits, drained and 1/2 c. juice reserved
1/3 c. brown sugar, packed
1/3 c. butter, melted
1 c. all-purpose flour
3/4 c. sugar
1/2 t. baking powder
1/4 c. butter, softened
1 egg, beaten
Garnish: maraschino cherries

Pat pineapple dry with paper towels. In a bowl, combine brown sugar and melted butter; divide mixture evenly into 12 greased muffin cups. Arrange pineapple chunks over brown sugar mixture. In a bowl, combine flour, sugar and baking powder. Mix in softened butter and reserved pineapple juice; beat for 2 minutes. Beat in egg. Spoon batter over pineapple, filling each cup 3/4 full. Bake at 350 degrees for 30 minutes, or until a toothpick tests clean. Cool in pan for 5 minutes. Place a wire rack on top of muffin tin and invert cupcakes onto rack so pineapple is on top. Cool completely and top each with a cherry.

Pineapple Upside-Down Cupcakes

Judy Lange, Imperial, PA

Ginger Ale Baked Apples

A yummy fall dessert or after-the-game snack!

Serves 4

4 baking apples
1/4 c. golden raisins, divided
4 t. brown sugar, packed and divided
1/2 c. ginger ale

Core apples but do not cut through bottoms. Place apples in an ungreased 8"x8" baking pan. Spoon one tablespoon raisins and one teaspoon brown sugar into center of each apple. Pour ginger ale over apples. Bake, uncovered, at 350 degrees, basting occasionally with ginger ale, for 45 minutes, or until apples are tender. Serve warm or cold.

Ginger Ale Baked Apples

Shar Toliver, Lillington, NC

Strawberry-Rhubarb Pie

The combination of strawberries and rhubarb is classic. This pie pairs the combination beautifully.

Makes 8 servings

5 c. strawberries, hulled and
    chopped
2 stalks rhubarb, peeled and diced
1/2 c. brown sugar, packed
1/2 c. sugar
1/4 c. all-purpose flour
2 T. cornstarch
1/2 t. cinnamon
9-inch pie crust
1-1/2 T. butter, diced

Combine strawberries and rhubarb; set aside. Sift together sugars, flour, cornstarch and cinnamon. Stir into strawberry mixture. Place crust in a 9" pie plate; chill for 10 minutes. Spoon strawberry mixture into crust; dot with butter. Sprinkle Crumb Topping over filling. Bake at 400 degrees for 50 to 60 minutes, or until topping is golden. Set pie on a wire rack to cool for 2 hours.

CRUMB TOPPING
3 T. all-purpose flour
1 T. sugar
1/8 t. salt
1 T. butter, softened

Mix together flour, sugar and salt; cut in butter until crumbly.

Strawberry-Rhubarb Pie

RELAX WITH DESSERT

Jodi Eisenhooth, McVeytown, PA

Pecan Cookie Balls

Make these sweet, crisp little morsels to go with an after-dinner cup of tea or coffee.

Makes 2-1/2 to 3 dozen

1 c. butter, softened
1 c. powdered sugar
2 c. chopped pecans
1 T. vanilla extract
2 c. all-purpose flour
4 T. powdered sugar

Blend together butter and powdered sugar; add pecans, vanilla and flour. Wrap dough in plastic wrap; chill for about 3 hours. Form dough into 3/4-inch balls; place on ungreased baking sheets. Bake at 350 degrees for 10 minutes. Let cool; roll in powdered sugar.

Pecan Cookie Balls

Lisa Thomsen, Rapid City, SD

Gail's Pumpkin Bars

These moist, full-of-flavor pumpkin bars are wonderful in the fall but are appreciated any time of year!

Makes 3 dozen

4 eggs, beaten
3/4 c. oil
1-1/2 c. sugar
15-oz. can pumpkin
2 c. all-purpose flour
2 t. baking powder
1 t. baking soda
1/2 t. salt
2 t. cinnamon
1/2 t. ground ginger
1/2 t. nutmeg
1/2 t. ground cloves

Mix together eggs, oil, sugar and pumpkin in a large bowl. Add remaining ingredients and mix well; pour into a greased and floured 18"x 12" jelly-roll pan. Bake at 350 degrees for 30 to 40 minutes, until a toothpick comes out clean. Let cool; frost with Cream Cheese Frosting and cut into bars.

CREAM CHEESE FROSTING
3 T. light cream cheese, softened
1 T. butter
2 T. milk
1 t. vanilla extract
2 c. powdered sugar

Beat together cream cheese, butter, milk and vanilla; gradually stir in powdered sugar and mix until spreading consistency.

Gail's Pumpkin Bars

Tiffany Leiter, Midland, MI

Speedy Peanut Butter Cookies

That's correct...there's no flour in these cookies!

Makes 12 to 15

1 c. sugar
1 c. creamy peanut butter
1 egg, beaten

Blend ingredients together; set aside for 5 minutes. Scoop dough with a small ice cream scoop; place 2 inches apart on ungreased baking sheets. Make a crisscross pattern on top of each cookie using the tines of a fork; bake at 350 degrees for 10 to 12 minutes. Cool on baking sheets for 5 minutes; remove to wire rack to finish cooling.

Cynthia Dodge, Layton, UT

Chocolate-Orange Zucchini Cake

This chocolate cake is a work of art! It is so moist and rich and will become the cake they always ask for!

Serves 12

1/2 c. plus 2 T. baking cocoa, divided
2-1/2 c. plus 2 T. all-purpose flour, divided
1/2 c. butter
2 c. sugar
3 eggs
2 t. vanilla extract
zest of 1 orange
1/2 c. milk
3 T. canola oil
3 c. zucchini, peeled and shredded
2-1/2 t. baking powder
1-1/2 t. baking soda
1/2 t. salt
1/2 t. cinnamon
Garnish: baking cocoa

Spray a 10-inch Bundt® pan with non-stick vegetable spray. Mix 2 tablespoons cocoa with 2 tablespoons flour. Coat interior of pan with mixture; shake out any extra and set aside pan. In a large bowl, beat butter and sugar with an electric mixer on medium speed. Add eggs, one at a time, beating well after each addition. Stir in vanilla, orange zest and milk. In a separate bowl, combine remaining cocoa and oil; mix thoroughly. Add cocoa mixture to butter mixture; stir well. Fold in zucchini. Add remaining flour and other ingredients. Beat on low speed until well blended. Pour into prepared pan. Bake at 350 degrees for about one hour, until a wooden toothpick tests clean. Cool in pan for 10 minutes; remove from pan to a cake plate. Cool completely. Dust top of cake with baking cocoa.

Chocolate-Orange Zucchini Cake

Melanie Lowe, Dover, DE

Cinnamon Poached Pears

You'll love this light dessert that's not too sweet.

Serves 4

4 pears
1 c. pear nectar
1 c. water
3/4 c. maple syrup
2 4-inch cinnamon sticks, slightly
    crushed
4 strips lemon zest

Peel and core pears from the bottom, leaving stems intact. Cut a thin slice off bottom so pears will stand up; set aside. Combine remaining ingredients in a saucepan. Bring to a boil over medium heat, stirring occasionally. Add pears, standing right-side up. Reduce heat and simmer, covered, for about 20 to 30 minutes, until tender. Remove pears from pan. Continue to simmer sauce in pan until reduced to 3/4 cup, about 15 minutes. Serve pears drizzled with sauce.

Cinnamon Poached Pears

Becky Smith, North Canton, OH

Royal Strawberry Shortcake

This recipe was passed down from my Grandma Emma. This stack of yummy strawberries and cake is a special treat...and so beautiful.

Serves 12

1/4 c. butter
1/2 c. sugar
1 egg, beaten
2 c. all-purpose flour
4 t. baking powder
1/8 t. salt
1 c. milk
2 t. vanilla extract
4 c. strawberries, hulled and sliced
Garnish: light whipped topping,
    powdered sugar

In a large bowl, blend together butter and sugar. Add egg; mix well. In a separate bowl, combine flour, baking powder and salt. Add flour mixture to butter mixture alternately with milk. Stir in vanilla. Spread batter in a greased 13"x9" baking pan. Bake at 350 degrees for 25 to 30 minutes. Cool; cut shortcake into squares and split. Place bottom layers of shortbread squares on dessert plates. Top with strawberries and one tablespoon whipped topping. Add top layers and more whipped cream and strawberries. Serve immediately.

Royal Strawberry Shortcake

Allison May, Seattle, WA

Lemon Chess Bars

These delicious bars freeze well...
keep some on hand to serve to
unexpected guests!

Makes 16

1/2 c. butter, softened
1 c. plus 2 T. all-purpose flour, sifted
   and divided
1/4 c. powdered sugar
2 eggs
1 c. sugar
zest of 1 lemon
3 T. lemon juice
Garnish: additional powdered sugar

Place butter in a bowl and beat with
an electric mixer at medium speed
until fluffy. Add one cup flour and
1/4 cup powdered sugar and beat well.
Spoon into an ungreased 8"x8" baking
pan and press firmly. Bake at
325 degrees for 20 minutes.
Meanwhile, combine eggs, sugar,

remaining flour, lemon zest and
lemon juice in a bowl. Mix well;
pour over baked bottom layer. Bake
25 more minutes, or until center is
set. Cool. Sprinkle with powdered
sugar. Cut into bars.

Terri Lock, Waverly, MO

Charlotte's Chocolate Sheet Cake

My mother-in-law is famous
for this cake in our family...all
22 grandchildren request it when
we get together.

Makes 24 servings

3/4 c. butter
1 c. water
1/4 c. baking cocoa
2 c. all-purpose flour
1 c. sugar
1 t. baking soda
1/8 t. salt
1/2 c. buttermilk
2 eggs, beaten
Optional: chocolate frosting

Place butter, water and cocoa in a
saucepan. Heat until butter melts; let
cool. In a mixing bowl, combine flour,
sugar, baking soda and salt; mix well.
Add butter mixture, buttermilk
and eggs to flour mixture; stir
well. Spread in a greased 15"x10" jelly-
roll pan. Bake at 400 degrees for
20 minutes. Drizzle with chocolate
frosting if desired.

Lemon Chess Bars

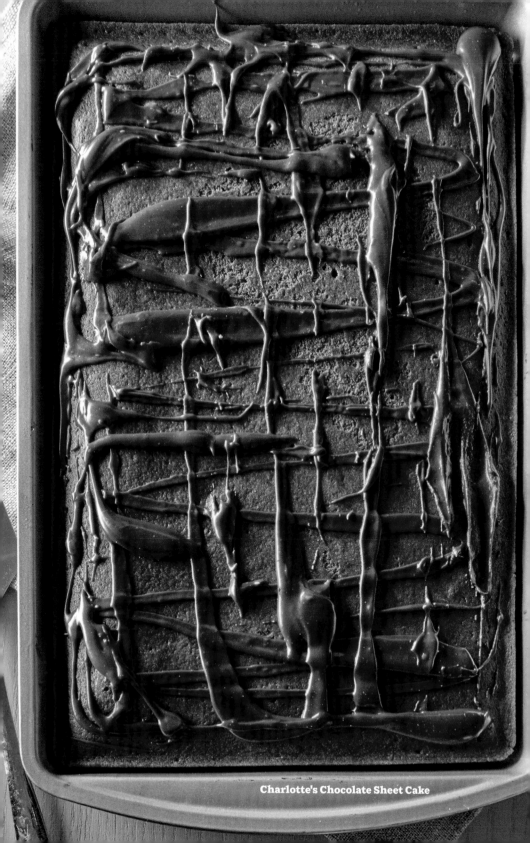
Charlotte's Chocolate Sheet Cake

Sharon Levandowski, Hoosick Falls, NY

Gram's Zucchini Cookies

Who would think zucchini would make these cookies so yummy?

Makes 4 dozen

3/4 c. butter, softened
1-1/2 c. sugar
1 egg, beaten
1 t. vanilla extract
1-1/2 c. zucchini, grated
2-1/2 c. all-purpose flour
2 t. baking powder
1 t. cinnamon
1/2 t. salt
1 c. chopped walnuts or almonds
6-oz. pkg. semi-sweet chocolate
    chips

Blend together butter and sugar in a bowl; beat in egg and vanilla. Stir in zucchini. In a separate bowl, combine flour, baking powder, cinnamon and salt; gradually add to butter mixture. Stir in nuts and chocolate chips.

Drop by heaping teaspoonfuls onto greased baking sheets. Bake at 350 degrees for 13 to 15 minutes, until golden. Remove to wire racks to cool.

Leona Krivda, Belle Vernon, PA

No-Bake Yummy Balls

This is a yummy, quick toss-together snack. The grandkids really like them, and my hubby & I love them with a cup of coffee. And they are healthy!

Makes 2 dozen

1-1/2 c. sweetened flaked coconut,
    toasted and divided
1 c. quick-cooking oats, uncooked
1/2 c. creamy peanut butter
1/3 c. honey
1/4 c. ground flax seed
1/4 c. wheat germ
1/4 c. mini semi-sweet chocolate
    chips
1/4 c. chopped walnuts
2 T. dried cranberries or cherries,
    chopped
1 t. vanilla extract

Combine 2/3 cup coconut and remaining ingredients in a bowl. Mix well with your hands. If mixture is too dry, a little more honey or peanut butter may be added. Roll into one-inch balls, then roll in remaining coconut. Place in an airtight container; cover and keep chilled.

Gram's Zucchini Cookies

No-Bake Yummy Balls

Index

Appetizers

Cheddar-Chive Bites, p204
Cheesy Spinach-Stuffed Mushrooms, p208
Cheese Quesadillas, p210
Cheesy Tuna Melts, p212
Chicken-Salsa Dip, p220
Cinnamon Crisps, p132
Cucumber & Salmon Rounds, p222
Greek Pita Pizza, p210
Honey-Glazed Snack Mix, p134
Market Veggie Triangles, p222
Mini Pizzas, p208
Pecan-Stuffed Deviled Eggs, p206
Pepperoni Pizza Sandwiches, p218
Pinwheel Starters, p214
Spicy Hummus, p206
Tangy Radish Bites, p216
Tiny Taco Beef, p216
Yummy Snack Mix, p214

Beverages

Banana-Mango Soy Smoothies, p54
Blueberry Flaxseed Smoothies, p32
Chai Tea, p152
Cranberry Tea, p148
Cucumber-Lime Agua Fresca, p220
English Cider, p144
Frosty Orange Juice, p48
Island Chiller, p212
Maple Hot Chocolate, p36
Mocha Coffee, p140
Raspberry Cream Smoothies, p52
Raspberry Punch, p204
Strawberry Preserves Smoothies, p66
Summertime Iced Tea, p218
Warm Spiced Milk, p132

Breads

Apple & Walnut Scones, p128
Bacon-Corn Muffins, p30
Blueberry Scones, p54
Buttermilk Cinnamon Rolls, p128
Cheese & Basil Scones, p44
Chocolate Pinwheels, p132
Cranberry Applesauce Muffins, p10
Crispy Corn Fritters, p178
Delicious Dill Bread, p156
Delicious Quick Rolls, p162
Easy Banana Bread, p126
Ginger-Carrot Bread, p138
Glazed Pumpkin Scones, p142
Gorilla Bread, p146
Grandma's Tomato Muffins, p120
Granny's Country Cornbread, p38
Kelly's Easy Caramel Rolls, p140
Lemon-Rosemary Zucchini Bread, p26
Maple-Walnut Muffins, p46
Mile-High Biscuits, p64
Mini Pumpkin Spice Loaves, p50
Orange Coffee Rolls, p152
Peanut Butter Muffins, p22
Roquefort Cut-Out Crackers, p100
Rosemary-Lemon Scones, p136
Sour Cream Mini Biscuits, p190
Southwestern Flatbread, p56
Sweet Fruit & Almond Scones, p148
Sweet Potato Cornbread, p42
Whole-Wheat Soda Bread, p136

Breakfast

After-Church Egg Muffins, p8

Apple Pie Oatmeal, p8

Best-Ever Breakfast Bars, p24

Blueberry-Lemon Crepes, p10

Blueberry Pillows, p18

Breakfast Berry Parfait, p36

Breakfast Spinach Quiche, p50

Breezy Brunch Skillet, p30

California Omelet, p12

Cheese & Chive Scrambled Eggs, p12

Cinnamon-Pumpkin Pancakes, p14

Cranberry Hootycreek Pancakes, p20

Egg Casserole Deluxe, p34

Farm-Fresh Omelet, p60

Fluffy Baked Eggs, p16

French Toast Casserole, p48

Good Morning Chile Relleno, p46

Grab & Go Breakfast Cookies, p16

Grandma McKindley's Waffles, p18

Ham & Gruyère Egg Cup, p56

Hearty Breakfast Quinoa, p40

Herbed Mushroom Omelets, p42

Herbed Sausage Quiche, p28

Johnny Appleseed Toast, p58

Light & Fluffy Pancakes, p38

Lizzy's Make-Ahead Egg Casserole, p64

Mini Breakfast Pizza, p66

Oatmeal Waffles, p62

Orange Yogurt Pancakes, p44

PB & J Oatmeal, p58

Peanut Butter French Toast, p28

Peggy's Granola, p52

Potato-Egg Bake, p60

Puffy Pear Pancake, p40

Red Velvet Pancakes, p26

Rise & Shine Sandwiches, p24

Stir & Go Biscuits & Sausage Gravy, p32

Strawberry-Hazelnut Grits, p34

Sunrise Granola, p20

Texas Toads in the Hole, p14

Veggie & Cheddar Crustless Quiche, p62

Warm Country Gingerbread Waffles, p22

Desserts

Apple Bread Pudding, p232

Blackberry Buckle, p126

Blue-Ribbon Pecan Pie, 230

Break-of-Day Berry Parfait, p130

Butter Pecan Peach Cake, p232

Can't-Be-Beet Cake, p226

Charlotte's Chocolate Sheet Cake, p246

Chocolate Cappuccino Brownies, p230

Chocolate-Orange Zucchini Cake, p242

Cinnamon Poached Pears, p244

Cranberry-Pecan Coffee Cakes, p134

Easy Apple Crisp, p226

Eva's Fruit Cobbler, p236

Gail's Pumpkin Bars, p240

Ginger Ale Baked Apples, p238

Grandmother's Waffle Cookies, p234

Gram's Zucchini Cookies, p248

Granny's Apple Coffee Cake, p130

Homemade Carrot Cake, p228
Lemon Chess Bars, p246
Maple-Pecan Brunch Ring, p142
Miss Karen's Coffee Cake, p144
No-Bake Yummy Balls, p248
Orange & Walnut Brunch Cake, p138
Peach Cobbler Cupcakes, p146
Peach Melba Pie, p228
Pecan Cookie Balls, p240
Pineapple Upside-Down Cupcakes,
   p236
Pumpkin Spice Bars, p150
Speedy Peanut Butter Cookies, p242
Strawberry-Rhubarb Pie, p238
Royal Strawberry Shortcake, p244
Taffy Apple Pizza, p150
The Best Oatmeal Cookies, p234

Mains-Beef

Beef & Asparagus Toss, p158
Beef & Noodle Skillet, p160
Chicken-Fried Steak, p168
Classic Beef Pot Roast, p186
Cranberry Meatloaves, p192
Gramma's Smothered Swiss Steak,
   p174
Ground Beef & Kale Curry, p164
Mongolian Beef, p176
One-Pot Spaghetti, p188
Poor Man's Steak & Vegetables, p190
Savory Herb Roast, p194
South-of-the-Border Squash Skillet,
   p180

Mains-Fish & Seafood

Firecracker Grilled Salmon, p192
Gingered Shrimp & Snow Peas, p90

Mains-Pork

Apple Spice Country Ribs, p196
BLT Kabobs, p164
Blue-Ribbon Corn Dog Bake, p92
Herbed Pork Ribeye Roast with
   Cauliflower, p166
Herbed Sausage Quiche, p96
Sam's Sweet-and-Sour Pork, p182
Skillet Apples & Pork Chops, p170

Mains-Poultry

Creamy Chicken & Biscuits, p160
Dijon Chicken & Fresh Herbs, p172
Good & Healthy "Fried" Chicken, p156
Santa Fe Chicken & Potatoes, p168
Slow-Cooker Country Chicken &
   Dumplings, p184

Mains-Vegetarian

3-Cheese Pasta Bake, p162
Broccoli Quiche Peppers, p190
Crustless Spinach Quiche, p110
Eggplant Ratatouille, p158
Grilled Veggie Combo, p84
Herbed Zucchini & Bowties, p80
Mexican Coffee Cup Scramble, p106
Ricotta Gnocchi, p196
Stewed Lentils with Tomatoes, p98
Vegetable Quinoa Patties, p116
Zucchini Fritters, p174

Salads & Sides

Apple-Walnut Chicken Salad, p98

Arugula & Nectarine Salad, p80

Carrot-Raisin Salad, p108

Cheesy Chile Rice, p180

Chicken Taco Salad, p76

Chilled Apple & Cheese Salad, p76

Confetti Corn & Rice Salad, p82

Corn Pudding, p184

Country Cabin Potatoes, p186

Creamy Bacon & Herb Succotash, p198

Greek Salad, p120

Green Peas with Crispy Bacon, p194

Grilled Chicken Salad, p78

Honeyed Fruit & Rice, p112

Jolene's Chickpea Medley, p94

Penne & Goat Cheese Salad, p178

Quick & Easy Veggie Salad, p86

Quinoa Tabbouleh, p108

Reuben Tossed Salad, p118

Santa Fe Vegetable Salad, p112

Simple Scalloped Tomatoes, p176

Spicy Roasted Potatoes, p198

Spring Ramen Salad, p74

Sunflower Strawberry Salad, p116

Suzanne's Tomato Melt, p122

Sweet Ambrosia Salad, p78

Tomato Salad with Grilled Bread, p114

Sandwiches

Buffalo Chicken Salad Sliders, p70

Caesar Focaccia Sandwich, p82

Cherry Tomato Hummus Wraps, p72

Delicious BBQ Hamburgers, p110

Egg Bagel Sandwich, p90

Grilled Chicken & Zucchini Wraps, p70

Grilled Havarti Sandwiches, p86

Grilled Veggie Sandwich, p94

Lucy's Sausage Salad, 88

Mediterranean Sandwiches, p72

Midwestern Pork Tenderloin Sandwich, p170

Monte Cristo Denver, p102

Nacho Burgers, p92

Peanut Butter Apple-Bacon Sandwich, p118

Pepper Steak Sammie, p104

Tomato Sandwiches, p112

Soups & Stews

Beefy Harvest Soup, p182

California Avocado Soup, p74

Chilled Melon Soup, p88

Colorful Fruit Soup, p106

Cream of Asparagus Soup, p104

Garbanzo Bean Soup, p122

Grandma's Pastina, p84

Pumpkin Chowder, p114

Quick & Easy Tomato Soup, p100

Sausage Bean Gumbo, p96

Slow-Cooker Butternut Squash Soup, p188

Slow-Cooker Steak Chili, p200

Whole Acorn Squash Cream Soup, p172

U.S. to Metric Recipe Equivalents

Volume Measurements

1/4 teaspoon . . . . 1 mL
1/2 teaspoon . . . . 2 mL
1 teaspoon. . . . . 5 mL
1 tablespoon = 3 teaspoons . . . . 15 mL
2 tablespoons = 1 fluid ounce . 30 mL
1/4 cup . . . . 60 mL
1/3 cup . . . . 75 mL
1/2 cup = 4 fluid ounces . . . . 125 mL
1 cup = 8 fluid ounces. . . . . 250 mL
2 cups=1 pint=16 fluid ounces 500 mL
4 cups = 1 quart . . . . 1 L

Weights

1 ounce. . . . . 30 g
4 ounces . . . . 120 g
8 ounces . . . . 225 g
16 ounces = 1 pound . . . . 450 g

Baking Pan Sizes

Square

8x8x2 inches . . . . 2 L = 20x20x5 cm
9x9x2 inches . . . . 2.5 L = 23x23x5 cm

Rectangular

13x9x2 inches. . . . . 3.5 L = 33x23x5 cm

Loaf

9x5x3 inches . . . . 2 L = 23x13x7 cm

Round

8x1½ inches. . . . . 1.2 L = 20x4 cm
9x1½ inches. . . . . 1.5 L = 23x4 cm

Recipe Abbreviations

t. = teaspoon . . . . ltr. = liter
T. = tablespoon. . . . . oz. = ounce
c. = cup. . . . . lb. = pound
pt. = pint . . . . doz. = dozen
qt. = quar . . . . pkg. = package
gal. = gallon . . . . env. = envelope

Oven Temperatures

300° F . . . . 150° C
325° F . . . . 160° C
350° F. . . . . 180° C
375° F. . . . . 190° C
400° F . . . . 200° C
450° F. . . . . 230° C

Kitchen Measurements

A pinch = 1/8 tablespoon
1 fluid ounce = 2 tablespoons
3 teaspoons = 1 tablespoon
4 fluid ounces = 1/2 cup
2 tablespoons = 1/8 cup
8 fluid ounces = 1 cup
4 tablespoons = 1/4 cup
16 fluid ounces = 1 pint
8 tablespoons = 1/2 cup
32 fluid ounces = 1 quart
16 tablespoons = 1 cup
16 ounces net weight = 1 pound
2 cups = 1 pint
4 cups = 1 quart
4 quarts = 1 gallon